The Complete Keto Meal Prep Cookbook

200 Recipes and a Weekly Meal Prep Plan

Written by: Jamie Stewart

Warning-Disclaimer

The purpose of this book is to educate and entertain. The author or publisher does not guarantee that anyone following the techniques, directions, tips, ideas, or strategies will achieve the same results. The author and publisher shall have neither liability or responsibility to anyone with respect to any loss or damage caused, or alleged to be caused, directly or indirectly by the information contained in this book.

Contents

INTRODUCTION

The human body must be supplied with a building material or essential nutrients, which are needed for its growth, cell regeneration, and normal daily activities. Eating well and losing weight can feel like a difficult goal for most of us. However, it doesn't have to be that way because there are so many go-to tricks and ideas for healthy eating at home.

As you are probably aware, there is no "one-size fits all" solution; however, there are some eating rules almost all nutritionists and physicians agree on. Start every day with breakfast, stay hydrated, get enough sleep, forget junk food and stop dieting are some of general rules that most of us often hear. It's a no-brainer that you can easily adopt healthy eating habits, boost your energy naturally and drop the pounds in the process. Meal prep is the secret of healthy, happy and skinny people! Improve your life with meal planning, embrace healthy eating habits and drop a dress size while saving your time and money!

If you want to achieve a well-balanced diet, home-cooked meals are the best choice. Researches have shown that families who cook at home are more likely to meet nutritional requirements. On the other hand, studies have shown that fast food that is low in nutritional value and high in calories contributes to the obesity problems. In fact, obesity is linked to a range of diseases such as arthritis, type 2 diabetes, cardiovascular disease, and so on.

Cooking at home and meal prepping may seem daunting and overwhelming. Yes, it's true, making time to cook at home requires self-discipline and knowledge; it's not easy, but it's possible. However, this cookbook is comprehensive enough to teach anyone about meal prep, making it easy and achievable. Knowing is half the battle, right?!

Ten Meal Prep Tips from Top Nutritionists

Wouldn't it be nice if you were like some of the foodies and nutritionist who eat well all week? Their method is incredibly simple – it is meal prepping! In other words, you can prepare big batches of beans, proteins, and sauces and combine them for breakfast, brunch, lunch, and dinner. Cooking big batches of food that you can store in the refrigerator and freeze sounds like a great idea! Meal prep is the answer to controlling your diet! And it doesn't require a serious lifestyle change.

1. **Make a plan and stick to it.**
   Even the best plan will fail without proper action, right? Whether you cook full recipes or not, make sure to use common ingredients such as beans, rice, pasta, onions, or tomato sauce. Cooked chicken and vegetables can be Chinese-style stir-fry, Mexican tacos or Italian chicken cacciatore; just add a different combination of spices and sauces. On the other hand, you can use sautéed vegetables such as onion, peppers, garlic and mushrooms to make a stew for Monday, a frittata for Tuesday and veggie casserole for Wednesday. Along the way, you will discover your own hacks to make meal prep much easier!

   Just a few hours in the kitchen on the weekend can save you plenty of time, while providing you with enough healthy food that will last all week.

2. **Keep it simple.** Start with easy-to-follow recipes and one-pot meals; then, move to ones that are more complicated.

3. **You can start small and grow big.** By starting small, you can build great habits that eventually lead to the great results in the kitchen. Pick a few simple recipes with limited ingredients; your goal is to cook good, satisfying meals that can be frozen so you can use them during the week. Later, you can cook larger amount of foods and keep them in your freezer in the next 5 or 6 months.

4. **Cook meals you really want to eat.** This advice may sound silly but, honestly, you will be tempted to order pizza if you don't like the prepared meals. Doubling recipes can save you a lot of time and money; if you think you will end up eating the same food every day, open your mind and try the recipes from this collection.

5. **Look for cooking shortcuts.** If you don't have extra time on your hands, simply use rotisserie chicken and pre-cut veggies and fruits; buy canned beans and tuna. Use your food processor to chop veggies. Preheat your oven and roast vegetables and meat all at once to save time and money. Did you know that you could cook eggs in the oven? Place them in a muffin tin and bake at 325 degrees F for 30 minutes. It's super-easy!

6. **Buy in bulk.** In general, buying in bulk can save you tons of money. For example, when you are preparing meals for a few months, consider using a large amount of dry beans and lentils. Then, cook them all at once and divide between airtight containers. Later, in the next few months, you can defrost cooked beans and use them to make your chilies, salads, hummus, soups, and so on.

   As long as you store your foods properly, they can last for months. For those busy weeknights when you don't have the time to cook for your family, it is great to reach into the freezer for your favorite meals.

7. **Find good storage containers.** You should invest in good food containers of various sizes according to your personal preferences. If you opt for this lifestyle, you might want to think about good plastic containers with lockable lids that are BPA-free, oven-safe container sets, lunchboxes and even an insulated bag. You can buy glass containers that allow you to portion-size your meals effectively and you can eat from them too. In general, good takeout-style containers are worth their investment.

8. **Prepare your protein.** Proteins such as garbanzo beans, fish poultry or eggs will help cut down on individual cooking times. You can use them in sandwiches, salad bowls, casseroles, and so forth.

9. **Small is the new big.** To illustrate, instead of making a large meatloaf, opt for muffins! In this way, you don't have to thaw the whole portion. Further, you can make a large casserole-style dish and slice it into portions; place each portion in a separate container, so when you freeze them, they are already ready to go!

10. **Label your food for the freezer.** Any self-adhesive label will work. Make sure to add the date on which you made it.

Top Five Benefits of Meal Prepping

1. Making your health your top priority.
   The whole family can reap considerable benefits from meal prepping. If you make time to sit down at the dinner table and eat home-cooked meals, you set a great example for your children.

   Families who eat together are less likely to be overweight because you can control portion size and choose the ingredients you really want to eat; the average restaurant meal has as much as 50% more calories than a home-cooked meal. Cooking at home allows you to use local, seasonal and fresh ingredients without colors and preservatives. You will reduce the amount of sugar, salt and saturated fat too. You will be able to decrease the number of unhealthy ingredients in recipes without sacrificing the flavor. Instead of white rice and flour, you can try multigrain and whole meal varieties. Instead of unhealthy fats and oils, you can use monounsaturated fats such as olive or coconut oil.

   Studies have found that families who consume meals made at home regularly tend to be healthier and eat less processed foods. Finding time to eat with your family may reduce stress and anxiety as well. Families who eat together are also happier. Nothing can match it!

2. You'll improve your cooking life.
   How often do you cook at home? We all agree that home-cooked meals are much healthier than fast food. As soon as you take it seriously, you will start thinking about the easiest ways to improve your cooking life.

   There are many great ways to become a better home cook. You can take cooking classes, purchase many cookbooks, learn from the experts, watch cooking shows, and so on. If you want to make cooking feel faster and easier, meal prepping is perfect for you. You can cook big-batch recipes on the weekend and eat well for days and months.

   Our cookbook focuses on offering you a significant amount of recipes that are both healthy and easy to follow. The main purpose of writing this recipe collection is to make meal prepping easy and fun.

3. You can save your money on food but still eat well.
   Being well prepared before going to the grocery store is one of the best ways to stick to your food budget. Meal prepping and budgeting go hand in hand so it's important to buy the food you actually need and will use for preparing meals. Mark categories such as fruits, vegetables, frozen foods, and healthy fats. In this way, you will not be tempted to buy processed food or unnecessary sweets.

Further, if you decide to buy food in bulk, you can take advantage of your freezer. There is no need for frozen dinners when you already have homemade meals ready to be heated in your microwave. Right away! In addition, meal prepping can also benefit our environment by reducing our carbon footprint and electricity waste. There is really no excuse for not cooking.

4. You'll start losing weight fast.
   If you want to lose weight, you have to increase your metabolic rate. The easiest way to do that is to eat more nutrient-dense food and avoid processed food with lots of empty calories. To make a long story short, stop dieting once and for all! Skipping meals and restricting food will slow down your metabolism. It means that you should eat enough in order to boost your metabolism, feed your body and shed unwanted fat. Yo-yo dieters should be aware of serious health risks such as fatty liver, diabetes and heart disease. What is the solution?

   A much healthier approach to weight loss is to lose weight slowly and gradually by choosing homemade meals. Meal prepping is one of the most effective ways to balance your diet and lose weight because you are more likely to eat healthily when you already have a home-cooked meal in your refrigerator or freezer. It also means that you will be able to eliminate packaged foods so you will eat only fresh meals you've prepared. No boxes and cans, no more takeaway foods!

   For all these reasons, meal prepping has become increasingly popular as a health trend. Health and social benefits of meal prepping are fascinating!

5. Stress-free lifestyle and more free time.
   Learning about the right way to fuel your body and keep it healthy will lead to a stress-free lifestyle! For example, make a list of your favorite healthy foods; then, pick easy-to-follow recipes and make a plan; afterwards, prepare meals ahead of time and store them in your refrigerator or freezer. This method actually takes the hassle out of your life. You will not think about cooking every day and have a hard time deciding what to cook for busy nights.

   Is calorie counting stressing you out? With meal prep, you will have an automatic portion control; no need to count macronutrients and calories. In addition, every recipe in this cookbook has nutritional information and a number of serving sizes. Tracking macros is useful and it works for many people, but it shouldn't keep you from living. Remember – your eating habits should improve your life, they should not consume your life!

Basic Keto Diet Rules

A ketogenic diet is a low-carb, adequate-protein, and high-fat eating plan. The main goal of a ketogenic diet is to get into a state of ketosis. If you want to reach ketosis, you should avoid eating carbs; just keep your carb intake between 20 to 50 grams of net carbs per day. It means the fewer carbs you eat, the more effective results you get. When your body is in a fat-burning mode, it makes ketones to provide energy. In this way, your body burns fats rather than carbs and you will stay healthy and lose weight naturally.

Foods recommended on a ketogenic diet include:

- **Meat (preferably grass fed) – pastured poultry, pork, beef, goat, and veal.**
- **Fish & Seafood – catfish, tuna, haddock, salmon, shrimp, crab, etc.**
- **Non-starchy vegetables – broccoli, greens, celery, onions, leeks, cauliflower, cabbage, green beans, peppers, tomato, mushrooms, asparagus, and Brussels sprouts.**
- **Dairy products – whole milk, sour cream, heavy cream, unsweetened yogurt, cheese, kefir, and butter.**
- **Eggs**
- **Fats & Oils – olive oil, flaxseed oil, coconut oil peanut butter, and sesame oil.**
- **Sweeteners – Splenda, monk fruit powder, xylitol, erythritol, stevia, and yacon sweetener.**
- **Nuts and seeds – walnuts, almonds, macadamia nuts, sesame, sunflower, and pumpkin.**
- **Fruits – berries, apples, watermelon, peaches and avocado.**
- **Condiments – soy sauce, coconut aminos, mustard, pickles, fermented foods, vinegar, mayonnaise, and homemade sauces.**
- **Fermented soy products**
- **All kinds of spices and herbs**
- **Beverages – coffee, tea, lemonade**

Foods to avoid on a ketogenic diet include rice, grains, beans, starchy fruits, root vegetables processed food, and sugar. There are foods that are strictly off-limits and food that you can eat in moderation. With this in mind, you can easily start the ketogenic diet and achieve great results. "When a person goes on a keto diet, they lose a lot of weight. That's just what happens," says the New York City–based dietitian Kristen Mancinelli, RD.

Many surprising benefits come from a diet that focuses on a variety of wholesome, all-natural ingredients and low-carb foods. Healthy food choices lead to a healthy lifestyle that is free of stress, obesity and diseases. Certain studies tend to show that you can lose your weight and significantly improve the quality of your life on a keto diet. A ketogenic diet helps in treating and controlling diabetes, hyperglycemia, and Alzheimer's disease. It can also boost your mood naturally and improves your heart health. This dietary regimen may help reduce the risk of cancer as a suitable complementary treatment to chemotherapy and radiation.

A well-balanced diet and healthy food choices are key factors that contribute to your health and overall well-being. Ketogenic diet and meal prep go hand in hand because cooking homemade meals helps you limit processed foods and refined carbs. It is more about good eating habits rather than following strict dietary rules.

7- Day Kickstart Meal Plan

If you do not know where to start, here is an easy-to-use meal plan designed to make a keto diet and meal prep simple and enjoyable. During this first week, your aim should be to stay simple and eliminate cravings; so go slowly and focus on your goal.

You should plan ahead, so buy all the ingredients for all seven days before you begin. Begin every day with a good breakfast and smile! Feel free to start your day with a bulletproof coffee. Make your coffee with a teaspoon of butter or coconut oil. It may sound weird, but it is so delicious!

Stay hydrated and be sure to drink plenty of filtered water. You can add a slice of lemon or lime to your water. Keep a bottle of water and your lunch box with you during the day to avoid junk food temptation and stay on track.

Eat your breakfast around 7 a.m., lunch by 1 p.m. and dinner by 7 p.m. You will create a 6-hour gap between every meal as a kind of intermittent fasting. An intermittent fasting has several health benefits and it will increase your weight loss success.

Balance out the fats with the amounts of protein is extremely important on a keto diet. For the best results, avoid any type of desserts for the first two weeks. You can add sweetener or spices to your coffee and tea. Cinnamon, vanilla extract and stevia will work wonders for you and help you stop sugar cravings.

DAY 1
Breakfast – 2 hard-boiled eggs; 1slice of bacon; 1 slice of cheese
Lunch – Hot and Spicy Fish Stew; 1 serving of cauliflower rice; 1 large handful of lettuce
Dinner – Beef Sausage with Mayo Sauce

DAY 2
Breakfast – Scrambled Eggs; a dollop of sour cream; 1/2 of medium-sized avocado
Lunch – Pan-Seared Pork Steaks; 1 serving of tomato salad
Dinner – Roasted Asparagus with Feta Cheese

DAY 3

Breakfast – Genoa Salami and Vegetable Frittata; goat cheese (1 ounce)

Lunch – Sensational Chicken Wings with Broccoli, 1 serving of tomato salad

Dinner – Family Pizza with Spring Vegetables

DAY 4

Breakfast – Rich Dark Chocolate Smoothie

Lunch – Grilled Rib Eye Steak; 1 serving of coleslaw

Dinner – 1 grilled cod fillet; 1 serving of roasted carrots; a few slices of onion

DAY 5

Breakfast – Vegan Tofu Skillet

Lunch – 1 chicken breasts (grilled or roasted); 1 serving of cabbage salad

Dinner – 1 pork chop with mushrooms; greens with ketogenic vinaigrette

DAY 6

Breakfast – Omelet with veggies, 1 slice of hard cheese

Lunch – Creole Salmon Fillets

Dinner – Chinese-Style Turkey Meatballs; 1 serving of cauli rice

DAY 7

Breakfast – Sunday Vegetable Patties

Lunch – Chicken salad

Dinner – 1/2 chicken breast; Greek-style salad (tomato, cucumber, bell peppers, feta cheese)

Guide to Using This Cookbook

It's easy to create great family meals, save a ton of time in the kitchen and stay within a grocery budget if you plan ahead, use key time-saving ingredients, and have good and reliable recipes. Thus, this cookbook will be your steady kitchen companion. It contains two hundred recipes that are divided into seven main categories so you can explore a wide choice of dishes, from light and easy appetizers and sides to delectable desserts.

It is chock-full of hacks, cooking secrets, crafty tricks, innovations, and so forth. The recipes are written in an easy-to-follow way, guiding you every step of the way in order to prepare your food and save it for later. Moreover, every recipe contains the nutritional information so you can track your macronutrients. Let's get prepping!

COOKED FOODS

Recommended Storage Times

FOOD	MONTHS
Cooked meat	2-3
Ham, cooked	2
Meat dishes	2-3
Gravy & Meat broth	2-3
Fried chicken	4
Poultry, pieces covered with broth or gravy	6
Chicken nuggets, patties	1-3
Cooked poultry dishes	4-6
Meat soups & stews	2-3
Ham, fully cooked, whole	1-2
Ham, fully cooked, slices	1-2
Cooked fish	4-6
Vegetable soups & stews	2-3
Casserole, cooked	3

FOOD	MONTHS
Pasta, cooked	3
Rice, cooked	3
Baked bread & Rolls	2-3
Baked cake	2-3
Baked fruit pieces	6-8
Cheesecake	2-3
Baked muffins	6-12
Pancakes	3
Waffles	1
Ice cream	2

BREAKFAST

1. Genoa Salami and Vegetable Frittata

Ready in about 25 minutes
Servings 4

For weeknight dining, family gathering, or a rich Sunday breakfast, a frittata is always a good idea. Enjoy!

Per serving: 310 Calories; 26.2g Fat; 3.9g Carbs; 15.4g Protein; 1.9g Sugars

Ingredients

1/2 stick butter, at room temperature
1/2 cup scallions, chopped
2 garlic cloves, minced
1 serrano pepper, chopped
1 carrot, chopped
8 Genoa salami slices
8 eggs, whisked
Salt and black pepper, to taste
1/2 teaspoon dried dill weed

Directions

- Melt the butter in a pan that is preheated over a moderately high heat. Now, sauté the scallions for 4 minutes, stirring periodically.
- Add garlic and cook for 1 minute or until it is fragrant. Add serrano pepper and carrot. Cook an additional 4 minutes.
- Transfer the mixture to a baking pan that is lightly greased with a nonstick cooking spray. Top with salami slices.
- Pour the eggs over vegetables and salami; season with salt, pepper, and dill. Bake approximately 18 minutes. Let cool completely.

Storing

Cut the frittata into four wedges. Place each of them in an airtight container; place in the refrigerator for up 3 to 4 days. To freeze, place in separate Ziploc bags and freeze up to 3 months. To defrost, place in your microwave for a few minutes.

2. Dill Pickle, Cheese, and Cauliflower Balls

Ready in about 3 hours 15 minutes
Servings 6

Serve these balls with cocktails at your next party! They are kid-friendly too.

Per serving: 407 Calories; 26.8g Fat; 5.8g Carbs; 33.4g Protein; 1.5g Sugars

Ingredients

4 cups cauliflower rice
1/2 pound pancetta, chopped
6 ounces Cottage cheese, curds, 2% fat
6 ounces Ricotta cheese
1 cup Colby cheese
1/2 cup dill pickles, chopped and thoroughly squeezed
2 cloves garlic, crushed
1 cup grated Parmesan cheese
1/2 teaspoon caraway seeds
1/4 teaspoon dried dill weed
1/2 teaspoon shallot powder
Salt and black pepper, to taste
1 cup crushed pork rinds
Cooking oil

Directions

- Thoroughly combine cauliflower rice, pancetta, Cottage cheese, Ricotta cheese, Colby cheese, dill pickles, garlic, and 1/2 cup of grated Parmesan.
- Stir until everything is well mixed and shape cauliflower mixture into even balls. Now, transfer to your refrigerator for 3 hours.
- Now, in a mixing bowl, thoroughly combine the remaining 1/2 cup of Parmesan cheese, caraway seeds, dill, shallot powder, salt, black pepper and crushed pork rinds.
- Roll cheese ball in Parmesan mixture until they are completely coated.
- Then, heat about 1-inch of oil in a skillet over a moderately high flame. Fry cheeseballs until they are golden brown on all sides.
- Transfer to a paper towel to soak up excess oil. Let cool completely.

Storing

Transfer the balls to the airtight containers and place in your refrigerator for up to 3 days. For freezing, place in freezer safe containers and freeze up to 1 month. Defrost in the microwave for a few minutes.

3. Scrambled Eggs with Kale Pesto

Ready in about 15 minutes
Servings 4

This is one of the most nutritious breakfasts you'll ever eat on a keto diet. Eggs are loaded with high-quality protein, as well as 13 essential vitamins and minerals. Kale is packed full of vitamins, minerals, and fiber. Enjoy!

Per serving: 495 Calories; 45g Fat; 6.3g Carbs; 19.5g Protein; 1.6g Sugars

Ingredients

2 tablespoons ghee
8 eggs, well beaten
1/4 cup full-fat milk
Salt and ground black pepper, to your liking

For the Kale Pesto:
2 cups kale
1 cup parmesan cheese, grated
2 garlic cloves, minced
1/2 cup olive oil
2 tablespoons fresh lemon juice

Directions

- Melt the ghee in a heavy-bottomed sauté pan over moderately high heat. Whisk the eggs with milk, salt, and pepper.
- Now, cook this egg mixture, gently stirring, until the eggs are set but still moist and tender.
- Put all the ingredients for the pesto, except the olive oil, in your food processor or blender.
- Pulse until roughly chopped. With the machine running, slowly pour in the olive oil until you get the desired consistency.
- Serve over warm scrambled eggs. Let cool completely.

Storing

Divide scrambled eggs between four airtight containers or Ziploc bags. Refrigerate for up to 3 days. Put the prepared pesto in a separate containers keep in the refrigerator for a week.
For freezing, place scrambled eggs in four Ziploc bags and freeze up to 3 months. Defrost in the microwave for a few minutes.
Put the pesto in a separate Ziploc bag and freeze for up to a month; defrost overnight in your refrigerator.

4. Pancetta, Cheese and Egg Muffins

Ready in about 30 minutes
Servings 9

Here're scrambled egg muffins loaded with eggs, pancetta, and Monterey Jack cheese. Make sure not to overcook your muffins! You can have the best ingredients ever but an overcooked muffin is dry and tasteless.

Per serving: 294 Calories; 21.4g Fat; 3.5g Carbs; 21g Protein; 1.7g Sugars

Ingredients

9 slices pancetta
9 eggs
A bunch of scallions, chopped
1/2 cup Monterey Jack cheese, shredded
1/4 teaspoon garlic powder
1/2 teaspoon dried dill weed
Sea salt and ground black pepper, to taste

Directions

- Start by preheating your oven to 390 degrees F.
- Then, brush a 9-cup muffin pan with oil; line each cup with one slice of pancetta.
- In a mixing bowl, thoroughly combine the remaining ingredients.
- Divide the egg mixture among muffin cups. Bake in the preheated oven for 20 minutes. Let cool completely.

Storing

Place egg muffins in the airtight containers or Ziploc bags; keep in the refrigerator for a week. For freezing, divide egg muffins among three Ziploc bags and freeze up to 3 months. Defrost in your microwave for a couple of minutes. Bon appétit!

5. Mexican-Style Pan Pizza

Ready in about 15 minutes
Servings 2

With a killer crusty base and melt-in-your-mouth topping, this pizza is super quick to prepare and it is ideal for when you're just making two personal pizzas.

Per serving: 397 Calories; 31g Fat; 8.1g Carbs; 22g Protein; 3.1g Sugars

Ingredients

For the Crust:
4 eggs, beaten
1/4 cup sour cream
2 tablespoons flax seed meal
1 teaspoon chipotle pepper
1/4 teaspoon cumin seeds, ground
1/2 teaspoon dried coriander leaves
Salt, to taste
1 tablespoon garlic-infused olive oil

For the Toppings:
2 tablespoons tomato paste
2 ounces 4-cheese Mexican blend, shredded

Directions

- Thoroughly combine all ingredients for the crust, except for the oil.
- Heat 1/2 tablespoon of garlic-infused oil in a pan over moderately high heat. Now, spoon 1/2 of crust mixture into the pan and spread out evenly.
- Cook until the edges are set; then, flip the pizza crust and cook on the other side. Turn the broiler on high.
- Heat the remaining 1/2 tablespoon of oil in the pan. Repeat with another pizza crust. Spread tomato paste over the top of each of the prepared pizza crusts.
- Divide Mexican cheese blend among these two pizza crusts.
- Broil them on high until the cheese is completely melted. Let cool completely.

Storing

Cut the pizza into two pieces. Place each of them in an airtight container; place in the refrigerator for up to 3 to 4 days.
To freeze, place in separate Ziploc bags and freeze up to 3 months. Defrost in your microwave for a few minutes.

6. Easy Two-Cheese Omelet

Ready in about 15 minutes
Servings 2

Tomato is the perfect garnish to this omelet but you can use sour cream, pickles, and red onions as well.

Per serving: 307 Calories; 25g Fat; 2.5g Carbs; 18.5g Protein; 1.6g Sugars

Ingredients

4 eggs
Salt, to taste
1/4 teaspoon black peppercorns, crushed
1 tablespoon sesame oil
1/4 cup Blue Cheese, crumbled
1/4 cup Appenzeller cheese, shredded
1 tomato, thinly sliced

Directions

- Whisk the eggs in a mixing bowl; season with salt and crushed peppercorns.
- Heat the oil in a sauté pan over medium-low heat. Now, pour in the eggs and cook, using a spatula to swirl the eggs around the pan.
- Cook the eggs until partially set. Top with cheese; fold your omelet in half to enclose filling. Let cool completely.

Storing

Slice the omelet into two pieces. Place each of them in an airtight container or Ziploc bag; place in the refrigerator for up to 3 to 4 days.
To freeze, place in separate Ziploc bags and freeze up to 3 months. Defrost in your microwave for a few minutes. Bon appétit!

7. Easy and Yummy Scotch Eggs

Ready in about 20 minutes
Servings 8

This recipe for keto scotch eggs opens the door to endless possibilities. You can use sausage, lamb, pork or turkey meat. You can skip parmesan or use coconut flour. It is a good idea to wrap the eggs in smoked bacon or salami slices. Amazing!

Per serving: 247 Calories; 11.4g Fat; 0.6g Carbs; 33.7g Protein; 0.3g Sugars

Ingredients

8 eggs
1 ½ pounds ground beef
1/2 cup parmesan cheese, freshly grated
1 teaspoon granulated garlic
1/2 teaspoon shallot powder
1/2 teaspoon cayenne pepper
1 teaspoon dried rosemary, chopped
Salt and pepper to taste

Directions

- Boil the eggs until hard-cooked; peel them and rinse under cold, running water. Set aside.
- In a mixing bowl, thoroughly combine the other ingredients. Divide the meat mixture among 8 balls; flatten each ball and place a boiled egg on it.
- Shape the meat mixture around egg by using your fingers.
- Add the balls to a baking pan that is previously greased with a nonstick cooking spray.
- Bake in the preheated oven, at 360 degrees F for 18 minutes, until crisp and golden. Let cool completely.

Storing

Place scotch eggs in two airtight containers or Ziploc bags; keep in the refrigerator for up to 1 week. For freezing, divide them between two Ziploc bags; they can be frozen for up to 2 months. Defrost overnight and place in the oven at 175 degrees F for 10 minutes.

8. Zucchini Boats with Sausage and Eggs

Ready in about 35 minutes
Servings 3

Fresh zucchinis are loaded with sausage, mustard, and eggs. You can top these boats with grated cheese to finish.

Per serving: 506 Calories; 41g Fat; 4.5g Carbs; 27.5g Protein; 1.3g Sugars

Ingredients

3 medium-sized zucchinis, cut into halves
1 tablespoon deli mustard
2 sausages, cooked and crumbled
6 eggs
Salt, to taste
1/4 teaspoon black pepper, or more to taste
1/4 teaspoon dried dill weed

Directions

- Scoop the flesh from each zucchini halve to make shells; place zucchini boats on a baking pan.
- Spread the mustard on the bottom of each zucchini halve. Divide crumbled sausage among zucchini boats.
- Crack an egg in each zucchini halve, sprinkle with salt, pepper, and dill.
- Bake in the preheated oven at 400 degrees F for 30 minutes or until zucchini boats are tender. Let cool completely.

Storing

Place zucchini boats in three airtight containers or Ziploc bags; keep in your refrigerator for 3 to 4 days. Wrap each zucchini boat tightly in several layers of plastic wrap and squeeze the air out. Place them in a freezable container; they can be frozen for up to 1 month. Bake the thawed zucchini boats at 200 degrees F until they are completely warm.

9. Madras and Asparagus Cheesy Frittata

Ready in about 20 minutes
Servings 4

Enjoy this fresh from the oven frittata, inspired by Indian curry paste and freshly grated semi-hard American cheese.

Per serving: 248 Calories; 17.1g Fat; 6.2g Carbs; 17.6g Protein; 1.1g Sugars

Ingredients

2 tablespoons avocado oil
1/2 cup shallots, chopped
1 cup asparagus tips
8 eggs, beaten
1/2 teaspoon jalapeno pepper, minced
1 teaspoon Madras curry paste
Salt and red pepper, to your liking
3/4 cup Colby cheese, grated
1/4 cup fresh cilantro, to serve

Directions

- In an ovenproof frying pan, heat avocado oil over a medium flame. Now, sauté the shallots until they are caramelized.
- Add the asparagus tips and cook until they're just tender.
- Stir in the eggs, jalapeno pepper and Madras curry paste; season with salt and pepper. Now, cook until the eggs are nearly set.
- Scatter the cheese over the top of your frittata. Cook in the preheated oven at 375 degrees F for about 12 minutes, until your frittata is set in the middle. Let cool completely.

Storing

Cut the frittata into four wedges. Place each of them in an airtight container; place in the refrigerator for up 3 to 4 days. To freeze, place in separate Ziploc bags and freeze up to 3 months. To defrost, place in your microwave for a few minutes.

10. Classic Bacon Deviled Eggs

Ready in about 20 minutes
Servings 10

This is the classic recipe for deviled eggs with a little twist. Spicy, flavorful and mouthwatering, these bites are simply wonderful.

Per serving: 128 Calories; 9.7g Fat; 3.3g Carbs; 6.8g Protein; 1.1g Sugars

Ingredients

10 eggs
1/2 cup mayonnaise
1/4 cup cooked bacon, chopped
2 teaspoons lemon juice
1 tablespoon Marsala wine
2 teaspoons country-style Dijon mustard
1/4 teaspoon hot pepper sauce
Salt and red pepper flakes, to taste
Fresh dill weed sprigs, to serve

Directions

- Place the eggs in a single layer in a pan; cover with 2 inches of water.
- Bring to a boil over a high heat; now, reduce the heat and cook, covered, for 1 minute.
- Remove from heat and wait for 15 minutes; rinse.
- After that, peel the eggs and halve them lengthwise. Remove the yolks and mash them with a fork. Add mayonnaise, bacon, lemon juice, wine, mustard, and hot pepper sauce.
- Season with salt and crushed red pepper; mix until everything is well combined. Divide the mayonnaise-bacon mixture among egg whites.

Storing

Place deviled eggs in an airtight container or Ziploc bag; transfer to your refrigerator; they should be consumed within two days.
For freezing, spoon out the yolk mixture from the deviled eggs. Add the egg yolk mixture to an airtight container or Ziploc bag.
Place the container in the freezer for up to 3 months. To defrost, let them sit overnight in the refrigerator until they are fully thawed out.

11. Smoked Bacon Fries

Ready in about 15 minutes
Servings 6

Once you make these bacon fries, you won't need potato chips! Serve with salsa, ketchup or barbecue dip.

Per serving: 409 Calories; 31.6g Fat; 1.1g Carbs; 28g Protein; 0g Sugars

Ingredients

1 pound smoked bacon, cut into small squares
1 teaspoon mustard seeds
1 tablespoon paprika

Directions

- Preheat an oven to 360 degrees F.
- Bake smoked bacon for 12 to 15 minutes. Season with mustard seeds and paprika. Let cool completely.

Storing

Place bacon fries in an airtight container or wrap tightly with heavy-duty aluminum foil; transfer to your refrigerator; they should be consumed within 3 to 4 days.
To freeze, place in an airtight container and freeze up to 2 to 3 months. It has been thawed in the refrigerator and can be kept for an additional 3 to 4 days in the refrigerator before serving. Enjoy!

12. Spinach and Cheddar Breakfast Muffins

Ready in about 30 minutes
Servings 6

These savory muffins are a great choice for the perfect start to your busy day. Serve with fried bacon and enjoy!

Per serving: 252 Calories; 19.7g Fat; 3g Carbs; 16.1g Protein; 2.6g Sugars

Ingredients

1 cup full-fat milk
8 eggs
2 tablespoons vegetable oil
1/3 teaspoon salt
1/4 teaspoon ground black pepper, or more to the taste
1 cup spinach, chopped
1 ½ cups cheddar cheese, grated

Directions

- Preheat your oven to 350 degrees F.
- In a bowl, mix the milk, with eggs and oil. Add the remaining ingredients. Mix well to combine.
- Add the mixture to a lightly greased muffin tin.
- Bake for 25 minutes or until your muffins spring back when lightly pressed. Let cool completely.

Storing

Place these muffins in the airtight containers or Ziploc bags; keep in the refrigerator for a week.
For freezing, divide the muffins among three Ziploc bags and freeze up to 3 months. Defrost in your microwave for a couple of minutes. Enjoy!

13. Sunday Vegetable Patties

Ready in about 15 minutes
Servings 6

Cheddar is the perfect cheese for the low-carbohydrate kitchen. It works wonderfully with these patties. And remember – the harder the better!

Per serving: 153 Calories; 11.8g Fat; 6.6g Carbs; 6.4g Protein; 3.1g Sugars

Ingredients

2 medium-sized zucchinis, shredded
2 carrots, shredded
1 small-sized celery stalk, shredded
2 tablespoons parsley, chopped
1 white onion, finely chopped
1 garlic clove, finely minced
1 cup cheddar cheese, grated
2 tablespoons olive oil
1 egg yolk
Salt and black pepper, to taste
Lemon wedges, to serve

Directions

- Start by preheating your oven to 360 degrees F. Line a baking sheet with parchment paper.
- Now, press the shredded vegetables firmly to drain away the excess liquid. Then, thoroughly combine all ingredients, except for lemon wedges, in a mixing bowl.
- Shape the mixture into 12 patties and bake for 5 minutes per side. Let cool completely.

Storing

Place vegetable patties in three airtight containers or Ziploc bags; keep in the refrigerator for a week.
For freezing, divide them among three Ziploc bags and freeze up to 3 months. Defrost in your microwave for a couple of minutes. Enjoy!

14. Sour Cream and Chocolate Donuts

Ready in about 25 minutes
Servings 6

Forget fried and oily donuts like your grandma used to make. Try new-fashioned, fresh from the oven donuts! Sprinkle the glazed donuts with chopped hazelnuts or toasted coconut for a kid's birthday party.

Per serving: 218 Calories; 20g Fat; 10g Carbs; 4.8g Protein; 2.4g Sugars

Ingredients

2/3 cup coconut flour
1/4 cup xylitol
1 teaspoon baking powder
1/2 teaspoon baking soda
1 teaspoon cinnamon, ground
A pinch of salt
A pinch of ground cloves
1/2 stick butter, melted
1/2 cup sour cream
1 eggs
1 teaspoon pure vanilla extract

For the Frosting:
1 cup double cream
1 cup sugar-free chocolate, broken into chunks

Directions

- Begin by preheating your oven to 360 degrees F. Generously spritz a donut pan with a nonstick cooking spray.
- In a mixing bowl, thoroughly combine the coconut flour, xylitol, baking powder, baking soda, cinnamon, sea salt and cloves.
- In another mixing bowl, mix together the butter, sour cream, egg, and vanilla extract. Add the wet mixture to the dry mixture.
- Spoon the batter evenly into the donut pan. Bake approximately 17 minutes or until done.
- In the meantime, heat double cream in a pan over a moderate flame; let it simmer for 2 minutes.
- Fold in the chocolate chunks; mix until all the chocolate is melted. Frost your donuts. Let cool completely.

Storing

Place donuts in three airtight containers or Ziploc bags; keep in the refrigerator for a week.
For freezing, wrap the glazed donuts in foil before packing them into an airtight container. Place the container in the freezer for up to 3 to 4 months.
Thaw the donuts in the refrigerator. You can reheat them in an oven.

15. Fajita Beef Sausage with Vegetables

Ready in about 25 minutes
Servings 4

If you are searching for an authentic flavor, Fajita seasoning mix is the right choice for this skillet. Doubtless, Zahtar works well too.

Per serving: 227 Calories; 18g Fat; 9g Carbs; 7.1g Protein; 4g Sugars

Ingredients

1 tablespoon lard
2 smoked beef sausage links, sliced
1 teaspoon crushed garlic
2 zucchinis, sliced
1 carrot, sliced
1 teaspoon fajita seasoning
1 piquillo pepper, minced
2 bell peppers, sliced
1/2 teaspoon saffron

Directions

- Warm the lard in a wok that is preheated over a moderate heat.
- Now, brown chicken sausage along with garlic approximately 8 minutes.
- Add the other ingredients and cook, stirring periodically, for 13 minutes more. Let cool completely.

Storing

Place sausage and veggies in four Ziploc bags; keep in the refrigerator for a week.
For freezing, divide them among three Ziploc bags and freeze up to 3 to 4 months. Thaw them in the refrigerator. You can reheat the sausage and veggies in a pan. Enjoy!

16. Perfect Tuna Pâté

Ready in about 10 minutes + chilling time
Servings 12

Versatile and easy, this tuna pâté is a great idea for any occasion, from a luxury dinner party to the school lunch box. Serve with pickles or fresh vegetable sticks.

Per serving: 64 Calories; 2.9g Fat; 1.3g Carbs; 7.9g Protein; 0.2g Sugars

Ingredients

1 (14-ounce) tuna in brine, drained
1/2 cup Ricotta cheese
1/4 cup sour cream
2 tablespoons mayonnaise
1/2 teaspoon country Dijon mustard
2 ounces cilantro, finely chopped
Coarse salt and freshly cracked mixed peppercorns, to your liking
1/2 teaspoon smoked paprika

Directions

- Add all ingredients to a mixing bowl.
- Mix with a wide spatula until everything is well incorporated.
- Pour into a greased mold; chill for 6 hours or overnight.

Storing

Place tuna pâté in an airtight container; keep in the refrigerator for a week. You can freeze them in silicone molds.
Once frozen, unmold and put some wax paper between each little pâté to prevent them from sticking to each other. Now, place them in a freezer-safe container for up to 3 months. Thaw in your refrigerator.

17. Spring Sour Cream Omelet

Ready in about 15 minutes
Servings 2

When it comes to the perfect omelet recipe, it all boils down to versatility. You can invent your own fillings, savory and sweets. You can come up with your unique combo of seasonings. Or you can use leftovers from yesterday's lunch.

Per serving: 319 Calories; 25g Fat; 10g Carbs; 14.9g Protein; 4.4g Sugars

Ingredients

2 teaspoons butter
2 spring onions, chopped
2 spring garlic, chopped
4 eggs, beaten
1 (8-ounce) carton sour cream, divided
2 medium-sized tomatoes, sliced
1 piquillo pepper, minced
2 tablespoons chervil, chopped
Kosher salt and freshly ground black pepper, to taste

Directions

- Melt the butter in a pan that is preheated over a moderate flame. Sauté spring onion and garlic until they are just tender and fragrant.
- Then, whisk the eggs with sour cream. Add the egg mixture to the pan and gently smooth surface with a wide spatula; cook until the eggs are puffy and lightly browned on bottom.
- Place tomatoes, piquillo pepper and chervil on one side of the omelet. Season with salt and pepper.
- Fold your omelet in half. Let cool completely.

Storing

Slice the omelet into two pieces. Place each of them in an airtight container or Ziploc bag; place in the refrigerator for up 3 to 4 days.
To freeze, place in separate Ziploc bags and freeze up to 3 months. Defrost in your microwave for a few minutes.

18. Chocolate and Cashew Chia Pudding

Ready in about 35 minutes
Servings 4

Like a creamsicle but a little bit tastier! You can eat this chia pudding as a snack, breakfast or dessert.

Per serving: 93 Calories; 5.1g Fat; 9.2g Carbs; 4.4g Protein; 2.4g Sugars

Ingredients

3/4 cup cashew milk, preferably homemade
1/4 cup water
2 tablespoons almond butter
1/2 cup chia seeds
20 drops liquid stevia
1/2 teaspoon maple extract
3 tablespoons orange flower water
2 tablespoons cocoa powder, unsweetened

Directions

- Place cashew milk, almond butter, chia seeds, stevia, maple extract, orange flower water, and cocoa powder in a mixing bowl.
- Allow it to stand for 30 minutes, stirring periodically. Let cool completely.

Storing

Place chia pudding in four airtight containers; place in the refrigerator for up 3 to 4 days.
To freeze, place in separate containers and freeze up to 2 months. Thaw in the refrigerator before ready to serve.
You can make popsicles by adding the pudding into popsicle molds or little plastic cups.

19. Five-Minute Egg and Salami Breakfast

Ready in about 5 minutes
Servings 3

Breakfast in a mason jar? Don't believe in words and try this EGGcellent recipe.

Per serving: 303 Calories; 22.4g Fat; 3.6g Carbs; 21.6g Protein; 2.2g Sugars

Ingredients

3 teaspoons butter, melted
6 eggs
1/2 cup American yellow cheese, shredded
1/2 cup cottage cheese
3 slices Genoa salami, chopped
Coarse salt and ground black pepper, to taste
1 teaspoon yellow mustard

Directions

- Grease 3 mason jars with melted butter.
- Crack two eggs into each jar. Divide the other ingredients among the two jars.
- Cover and shake until everything is well incorporated.
- Remove lids and microwave for 2 minutes on high. Let cool completely.

Storing

Place the mixture in three airtight containers; keep in the refrigerator for up 3 to 4 days.
To freeze, place in separate Ziploc bags and freeze up to 3 months. Defrost in your microwave for a few minutes.

20. Smoked Bacon and Gorgonzola Muffins

Ready in about 25 minutes
Servings 5

The aroma of smoked bacon mixed with eggs and cheese is enough to make anyone salivate. It is perfect for Sunday breakfast or served as finger food at a cocktail party.

Per serving: 240 Calories; 15.3g Fat; 10g Carbs; 16.1g Protein; 0.4g Sugars

Ingredients

4 slices smoked back bacon
4 eggs, beaten
1/2 cup coconut flour
1 teaspoon baking powder
1 cup gorgonzola cheese, diced
A pinch of kosher salt
A pinch of grated nutmeg

Directions

- Preheat a frying pan over a moderately high heat. Now, cook the bacon, turning with tongs, until it is crisp and browned on both sides; drain your bacon on paper towels.
- Chop the bacon and combine it with the other ingredients; stir to combine well.
- Grease muffin molds. Fill the prepared molds with batter (3/4 full). Bake in the preheated oven at 390 degrees F for 15 minutes. Let cool completely.

Storing

Place these muffins in the airtight containers or Ziploc bags; keep in the refrigerator for a week.
For freezing, divide the muffins among three Ziploc bags and freeze up to 3 months. Defrost in your microwave for a couple of minutes. Enjoy!

21. Pancetta and Asiago Waffles

Ready in about 20 minutes
Servings 3

These waffles will melt in your mouth, we bet you won't miss the flour. You can even skip pancetta in this recipe.

Per serving: 453 Calories; 37g Fat; 4.5g Carbs; 25.6g Protein; 2.4g Sugars

Ingredients

6 large-sized eggs, separate egg whites and egg yolks
1/2 teaspoon baking powder
1/2 teaspoon baking soda
4 tablespoons ghee
Kosher salt, to taste
1/2 teaspoon dried oregano
3 tablespoons tomato paste
3 ounces pancetta, chopped
3 ounces Asiago cheese, shredded

Directions

- Thoroughly combine egg yolks, baking powder, baking soda, ghee, salt, and oregano in a mixing bowl.
- Now, beat the egg whites with an electric mixer until pale. Gently mix egg whites into the egg yolk mixture.
- Generously grease a waffle iron. Heat you waffle iron and pour in 1/4 cup of the batter. Cook until golden, about 3 minutes. Repeat until you run out of batter; you will have 6 thin waffles.
- Add one waffle back to the waffle iron; spread 1 tablespoon of tomato paste onto your waffle; top with 1 ounce of pancetta and 1 ounce of shredded cheese.
- Top with another waffle; cook until cheese is melted. Repeat with remaining ingredients. Let cool completely.

Storing

Place the waffles in the airtight containers or Ziploc bags; keep in the refrigerator for a week.
For freezing, divide the waffles among three Ziploc bags and freeze up to 3 months. Defrost in your microwave for a couple of minutes. Enjoy!

22. French-Style Strawberry Omelet

Ready in about 10 minutes
Servings 1

For an elegant touch, don't fail to add warmed cognac to finish. Crème de cassis and Grand Marnier (a French, orange-flavored liqueur) work well too.

Per serving: 488 Calories; 42g Fat; 8g Carbs; 15.3g Protein; 4.4g Sugars

Ingredients

2 eggs, beaten
2 tablespoons heavy cream
1/2 teaspoon ground cloves
1 tablespoon coconut oil
2 tablespoons cream cheese
6 fresh strawberries, sliced
1 tablespoon Cognac

Directions

- Whisk the eggs with heavy cream and ground cloves.
- Next, melt coconut oil in a pan that is preheated over medium-high heat. When hot, add the egg mixture; cook for about 3 minutes until the base is thoroughly cooked.
- Tip the omelet out onto a plate; top with cheese and strawberries. Roll it up; add warmed Cognac over your omelet and flambé. Let cool completely.

Storing

Slice the omelet into two pieces and place each of them in an airtight container or Ziploc bag; keep in your refrigerator for up 3 to 4 days.
To freeze, place in separate Ziploc bags and freeze up to 3 months. Defrost in your microwave for a few minutes. Bon appétit!

23. Crêpes with Butter-Rum Syrup

Ready in about 25 minutes
Servings 6

Is there anything better than the smell of fresh, homemade crepes on Sunday morning? Make these delicious and fluffy crepes from scratch, in less than 25 minutes, with common and easy-to-find keto ingredients.

Per serving: 243 Calories; 19.6g Fat; 5.5g Carbs; 11g Protein; 4.7g Sugars

Ingredients

For Crêpes:
6 ounces cream cheese, softened
6 eggs
1 ½ tablespoons granulated Swerve
1/4 cup almond flour
1 teaspoon baking soda
1 teaspoon baking powder
1/2 teaspoon apple pie spice mix

For the Syrup:
3/4 cup water
1 tablespoon butter
3/4 cup Swerve, powdered
1 tablespoon rum extract
1/2 teaspoon xanthan gum

Directions

- Combine all ingredients for the crepes using an electric mixer. Mix until everything is well incorporated.
- Grease a frying pan with melted butter; fry your crepes over a moderate heat until the edges begin to brown.
- Flip and fry on the other side until it is slightly browned.
- Whisk the water, butter, and Swerve in a pan over medium heat; simmer about 6 minutes, stirring continuously.
- Add the mixture to a blender along with rum extract and 1/4 teaspoon of xanthan gum; mix to combine.
- Add the remaining 1/4 teaspoon of xanthan gum and let it stand until the syrup is thickened. Let cool completely.

Storing

Place crepes in airtight containers or Ziploc bags; keep in your refrigerator for up 3 to 4 days.
To freeze, place a sheet of wax paper between each crepe and stack together. Wrap the tightly in aluminum foil. Freeze up to 1 to 2 months. Bon appétit!

24. Homemade Bread with Herbs and Seeds

Ready in about 40 minutes
Servings 6

Everyone loves the smell of homemade bread baking. It's simply adorable.
Cook's note: The dough shouldn't stick to your hands; if the dough is too sticky, just add more flour.

Per serving: 109 Calories; 10.2g Fat; 1g Carbs; 3.9g Protein; 0.2g Sugars

Ingredients

5 eggs, separated
1/2 teaspoon cream of tartar
2 cups almond flour
1/2 stick butter, melted
3 teaspoons baking powder
1 teaspoon sea salt
1 teaspoon dried basil
1/2 teaspoon dried oregano
1 tablespoon poppy seeds
2 tablespoons sesame seeds

Directions

- Preheat your oven to 360 degrees F. Lightly oil a loaf pan with a nonstick cooking spray.
- Mix the eggs with cream of tartar on medium-high speed until stiff peaks form.
- Add the flour, butter, baking powder and salt to your food processor; blitz until everything is well mixed.
- Now, stir in the egg white mixture; gently stir to combine well. Spoon the batter into the prepared loaf pan.
- Sprinkle dried basil, oregano, poppy seeds and sesame seeds on the loaf and bake for 35 minutes. Let cool completely.

Storing

For freezing, wrap the loaf with clear plastic bread bags. Freeze up to 2 months. To thaw the frozen bread, let it come to room temperature. Just before serving, place it in an oven heated to 400 degrees F for about 4 minutes.

25. Star Anise and Pecan Porridge

Ready in about 25 minutes
Servings 2

Porridge is an ultimate, everyday comfort food that is delicious and super easy to make. Turmeric is a powerful addition to this porridge – it has antioxidant and anti-inflammatory properties.

Per serving: 430 Calories; 41.1g Fat; 9.8g Carbs; 11.4g Protein; 6.5g Sugars

Ingredients

3 eggs
3 tablespoons Swerve
1/2 cup double cream
1 ½ tablespoons coconut oil
1/2 teaspoon star anise
1/4 teaspoon turmeric powder
1/4 cup pecans, chopped

Directions

- Thoroughly combine eggs with Swerve and double cream in a mixing bowl.
- Melt coconut oil in a pot over moderately high heat; stir in egg/cream mixture and cook until they are warmed through.
- Take off the heat and stir in star anise and turmeric. Add chopped pecans to the top. Let cool completely.

Storing

Divide the porridge into two portions; store each portion in an airtight container. Keep in the refrigerator for up to 5 days.
To freeze, place each portion in an airtight container; freeze for up to 3 months. Reheat the porridge in a microwave, stirring and adding some extra liquid if necessary. Bon appétit!

26. Fried Tofu with Peppers

Ready in about 40 minutes
Servings 2

Check out this creative recipe to turn any tofu block into something amazing! Be inspired and experiment with seasonings.

Per serving: 223 Calories; 15.9g Fat; 8.1g Carbs; 15.6g Protein; 2g Sugars

Ingredients

12 ounces extra firm tofu, pressed and cubed
1 ½ tablespoons flaxseed meal
Salt and ground black pepper, to taste
1 teaspoon garlic paste
1/2 teaspoon paprika
1 teaspoon shallot powder
1/2 teaspoon ground bay leaf
1 tablespoon olive oil
1 red bell pepper, deveined and sliced
1 green bell pepper, deveined and sliced
1 serrano pepper, deveined and sliced

Directions

- Place the tofu, flaxseed meal, salt, black pepper, garlic paste, paprika, shallot powder, and ground bay leaf in a container.
- Cover, toss to coat, and let it marinate at least 30 minutes.
- Heat olive oil in a saucepan over a moderate heat. Cook your tofu along with peppers for 5 to 7 minutes, gently stirring. Let cool completely.

Storing

Divide tofu between two airtight container or Ziploc bags; add peppers and keep in your refrigerator for up to 3 to 4 days.
To freeze, divide tofu into two pieces; place them along with peppers in two airtight container or Ziploc bags. Freeze up to 5 months. Defrost in the refrigerator. Enjoy!

27. Cilantro and Ricotta Balls

Ready in about 10 minutes + chilling time
Servings 6

Fun, easy and delicious, cheese balls are perfect for a party! In addition, these balls look spectacular on a serving platter.

Per serving: 108 Calories; 9g Fat; 2.2g Carbs; 4.8g Protein; 0.1g Sugars

Ingredients

1 cup Ricotta cheese
3 tablespoons butter
1/4 teaspoon red wine vinegar
Salt and pepper, to taste
1/2 cup fresh cilantro, finely chopped

Directions

- Blend all ingredients, except for cilantro, in a food processor.
- Place the mixture in the refrigerator for 3 hours.
- Shape the mixture into 10 to 12 balls; roll them in chopped cilantro until evenly coated. Let cool completely.

Storing

Divide ricotta balls between three airtight containers or Ziploc bags; keep in your refrigerator for up to 3 to 4 days.
For freezing, place ricotta balls in three airtight containers. Freeze up to 1 month. Defrost in the refrigerator. Enjoy!

28. Cheese, Mortadella and Salami Roll-Ups

Ready in about 10 minutes
Servings 5

It's not a party without these mellow roll-ups. This is an utterly addicting snack so consider preparing a double batch.

Per serving: 381 Calories; 31.2g Fat; 7.8g Carbs; 17.6g Protein; 1.7g Sugars

Ingredients

10 slices Provolone cheese
4 ounces mayonnaise
10 slices Mortadella
10 slices Genoa salami
10 olives, pitted

Directions

- Spread a thin layer of mayo onto each slice of cheese. Add a slice of Mortadella on top of the mayo.
- Top with a slice of Genoa salami. Roll them up; place olives on the top and secure with toothpicks.

Storing

Divide roll-ups between three airtight containers; keep in your refrigerator for up to 5 days.
For freezing, place roll-ups in three airtight containers. Freeze up to 3 months. Defrost in the refrigerator. Enjoy!

29. Paprika Provolone Crisps

Ready in about 15 minutes
Servings 6

Homemade keto snacks are a cinch to make. In addition, they are healthy and so delicious. Here's an amazing low carb snack that takes only 15 minutes to make.

Per serving: 268 Calories; 20.4g Fat; 3.4g Carbs; 18.1g Protein; 0.4g Sugars

Ingredients

3 cups provolone cheese, shredded
4 tablespoons ground flaxseed meal
1 teaspoon paprika powder

Directions

- Begin by preheating your oven to 420 degrees F.
- Then, drop a tablespoon of shredded cheese into 12 separate piles. Sprinkle ground flaxseed meal and paprika powder over the top.
- Bake in the middle of your oven for roughly 10 to 12 minutes. Let cool completely.

Storing

Divide crisps between two airtight containers or Ziploc bags; keep in your refrigerator for up to 4 days.
To freeze, divide crisps between two airtight containers. Freeze up to 2 months. Defrost and reheat in your oven until it is crisp. Enjoy!

30. Mini Salami Pizza Cups

Ready in about 20 minutes
Servings 6

A mild flavor of Cheddar cheese combines beautifully with the tanginess of marinara sauce and olives in this recipe.

Per serving: 162 Calories; 13.1g Fat; 2.5g Carbs; 8.7g Protein; 1.1g Sugars

Ingredients

1 cup Cheddar cheese, shredded
1/2 cup marinara
1 teaspoon dried oregano
1/2 teaspoon dried basil
1/2 cup green olives, pitted and chopped
12 Genoa salami slices

Directions

- Preheat an oven to 360 degrees F; spritz a muffin pan with a nonstick cooking spray.
- Divide 1/2 cup of cheddar cheese among muffin cups. Divide marinara sauce among muffin cups.
- Sprinkle each cup with oregano, basil, and chopped olives. Add a salami slice to each muffin cup. Top with the remaining 1/2 cup of cheese.
- Bake approximately 17 minutes. Allow them to cool slightly before removing from the muffin pan. Let cool completely.

Storing

Place pizza cups in the airtight containers or Ziploc bags; keep in the refrigerator for a week.
For freezing, divide pizza cups among three Ziploc bags and freeze up to 3 months. Defrost in your microwave for a couple of minutes. Enjoy!

31. Two Cheese Omelet with Pimenta and Chervil

Ready in about 15 minutes
Servings 2

An ultimate comfort food you deserve. Chervil will bring a fresh kick when added on top. You will go crazy for this breakfast!

Per serving: 490 Calories; 44.6g Fat; 4.5g Carbs; 22.7g Protein; 2.7g Sugars

Ingredients

2 tablespoons avocado oil
4 eggs, beaten
Salt and black pepper, to taste
1/4 teaspoon Pimenta, ground
1/4 teaspoon cayenne pepper
1/2 cup Asiago cheese
1/2 cup Boursin cheese
2 tablespoons fresh chervil, roughly chopped

Directions

- Heat the oil in a pan that is preheated over a moderately high heat.
- Season the eggs with salt, black pepper, ground Pimenta, and cayenne pepper. Add the seasoned eggs to the pan; tilt the pan to spread the eggs out evenly.
- Once set, top your eggs with cheese. Slice the omelet into two halves. Garnish with fresh chervil. Let cool completely.

Storing

Slice the omelet into two pieces and place each of them in an airtight container or Ziploc bag; keep in your refrigerator for up 3 to 4 days.
To freeze, place in separate heavy-duty freezer bags and freeze up to 3 months. Defrost in your microwave for a few minutes. Bon appétit!

32. Asiago and Sausage Egg Cups

Ready in about 10 minutes
Servings 3

Here's a perfect meal on-the-go! A smoked beef-pork sausage or Berliner sausage work well for these cups.

Per serving: 423 Calories; 34.1g Fat; 2.2g Carbs; 26.5g Protein; 0.9g Sugars

Ingredients

1 teaspoon butter, melted
6 eggs, separated into yolks and whites
Coarse salt and freshly ground black pepper, to taste
1/2 teaspoon smoked paprika
1/2 teaspoon dried sage
1 cup Asiago cheese, freshly grated
3 beef sausages, chopped

Directions

- Begin by preheating your oven to 420 degrees F. Lightly grease a muffin pan with melted butter.
- Now, beat the egg whites with an electric mixer until stiff peaks form. Add seasonings, cheese, and sausage.
- Pour into muffin cups and bake for 4 minutes.
- Now, add an egg to each cup. Bake for 4 more minutes. Leave the cups to cool down completely.

Storing

Place the egg cups in airtight containers; keep in the refrigerator for a week.
For freezing, divide the egg cups among three Ziploc bags and freeze up to 3 months. Defrost in your microwave for a couple of minutes. Enjoy!

33. Colby Cheese and Sausage Gofres

Ready in about 30 minutes
Servings 6

Don't overcook the eggs because they will come out dry and tasteless. These waffles should be fluffy and moist but not runny.

Per serving: 316 Calories; 25g Fat; 1.5g Carbs; 20.2g Protein; 1.2g Sugars

Ingredients

6 eggs
6 tablespoons whole milk
1 teaspoon Spanish spice mix
Sea salt and ground black pepper, to taste
3 fully-cooked breakfast sausage links, chopped
1 cup Colby cheese, shredded
Nonstick cooking spray

Directions

- In a mixing bowl, beat the eggs, milk, Spanish spice mix, salt, and black pepper.
- Now, stir in chopped sausage and shredded cheese.
- Spritz a waffle iron with a nonstick cooking spray.
- Cook the egg mixture about 5 minutes, until it is golden. Let cool completely.

Storing

Place your gofres in the airtight containers or Ziploc bags; keep in the refrigerator for a week.
For freezing, divide the gofres among three heavy-duty freezer bags; freeze up to 3 months. Defrost in your microwave for a couple of minutes. Enjoy!

34. Easy Breakfast Muffins

Ready in about 20 minutes
Servings 6

Who needs a cheese cake when you can have no-flour muffins loaded with cheese, nuts and fruits?

Per serving: 81 Calories; 3.5g Fat; 10.7g Carbs; 5.5g Protein; 8.4g Sugars

Ingredients

3/4 cream cheese
1/4 cup Greek-style yogurt
3 eggs, beaten
2 tablespoons hazelnuts, ground
4 tablespoons erythritol
1/2 teaspoon vanilla essence
1/3 teaspoon ground cinnamon
1 apple, cored and sliced

Directions

- Preheat your oven to 360 degrees F. Treat a muffin pan with a nonstick cooking spray.
- Then, thoroughly combine all of the above ingredients. Divide the batter among the muffin cups.
- Bake for 12 to 15 minutes. Transfer to a wire rack to cool slightly before serving. Garnish with apples. Let cool completely.

Storing

Divide muffins between two airtight containers; keep in the refrigerator for a week.
For freezing, divide the muffins among three Ziploc bags and freeze up to 3 months. Defrost in your microwave for a couple of minutes. Enjoy!

35. Chorizo and Ricotta Balls

Ready in about 15 minutes + chilling time
Servings 5

These easy and yummy balls made even heartier with cooked chorizo! Kalamata olives give the right amount of tanginess to the whole thing.

Per serving: 327 Calories; 25.7g Fat; 6.4g Carbs; 17g Protein; 1g Sugars

Ingredients

10 ounces chorizo, chopped
10 ounces Ricotta cheese, softened
1/4 cup mayonnaise
1/2 teaspoon deli mustard
2 teaspoons tomato paste
8 Kalamata olives, pitted

Directions

- Heat up the skillet over a moderate flame. Now, cook chorizo until well browned. Transfer it to a mixing bowl.
- Add the remaining ingredients and transfer to your refrigerator until it is well chilled.

Storing

Divide balls between three airtight containers or Ziploc bags; keep in your refrigerator for up 3 to 4 days. For freezing, place balls in three airtight containers. Freeze up to 1 month. Defrost in the refrigerator. Bon appétit!

36. Sopressata and Blue Cheese Waffles

Ready in about 20 minutes
Servings 2

These are the fluffiest waffle iron omelets in the world! If you don't have Sopressata on hand, you can use Pepperoni or leftover pork instead.

Per serving: 470 Calories; 40.3g Fat; 2.9g Carbs; 24.4g Protein; 1.7g Sugars

Ingredients

2 tablespoons butter, melted
Salt and black pepper, to your liking
1/2 teaspoon parsley flakes
1/2 teaspoon chili pepper flakes
4 eggs
1/2 cup blue cheese, crumbled
4 slices Sopressata, chopped

Directions

- Combine all ingredients, except for fresh chives, in a mixing bowl. Preheat your waffle iron and grease with a cooking spray.
- Add the omelet mixture and close the lid. Fry about 5 minutes or until desired consistency is reached. Repeat with the remaining batter. Let cool completely.

Storing

Place the waffles in separate airtight containers; keep in the refrigerator for a week.
For freezing, divide the waffles among two airtight containers or heavy-duty freezer bags and freeze up to 3 months. Defrost in your microwave for a couple of minutes. Enjoy!

37. Cheesy Cauliflower Fritters

Ready in about 35 minutes
Servings 6

Cauliflower fritters are SO versatile and SO easy to prepare! These fritters are actually loaded with two types of cheese, which add them an extra flavor and nutrition value. Enjoy!

Per serving: 199 Calories; 13.8g Fat; 7.8g Carbs; 13g Protein; 2.1g Sugars

Ingredients

1 ½ tablespoons olive oil
1 shallot, chopped
1 garlic clove, minced
1 pound cauliflower, grated
6 tablespoons almond flour
1⁄2 cup Swiss cheese, shredded
1 cup parmesan cheese
2 eggs, beaten
1/2 teaspoon dried dill weed
Sea salt and ground black pepper, to taste

Directions

- Heat the oil in a cast iron skillet over medium heat. Cook the shallots and garlic until they are aromatic.
- Add grated cauliflower and stir with a spatula for another minute or so; set aside to cool to room temperature so you can handle it easily.
- Add the remaining ingredients; shape the mixture into balls, then, press each ball to form burger patties.
- Bake in the preheated oven at 400 degrees F for 20 minutes. Flip and bake for another 10 minutes or until golden brown on top. Let cool completely.

Storing

Divide your fritters between two airtight containers or heavy-duty freezer bags; keep in the refrigerator for a week.
For freezing, divide the fritters among three heavy-duty freezer bags; freeze up to 3 months.
Defrost in your microwave for a few minutes. Bon appétit!

38. Spicy Sausage with Eggs

Ready in about 20 minutes
Servings 2

A rich and satisfying, this dish is guaranteed to make your meals so much better. Serve as a romantic breakfast on blustery winter days.

Per serving: 462 Calories; 40.6g Fat; 7.1g Carbs; 16.9g Protein; 1.1g Sugars

Ingredients

2 tablespoons olive oil
1/2 cup leeks, chopped
1 teaspoon smashed garlic
1 teaspoon habanero pepper, deveined and minced
Salt and black pepper to the taste
6 ounces sausage, crumbled
4 eggs, whisked
1 thyme sprig, chopped
1/2 teaspoon dried marjoram, chopped
1/2 cup ripe olives, pitted and sliced

Directions

- Heat the oil in a nonstick skillet over medium heat; now, sauté the leeks until they are just tender, about 4 minutes.
- Add the garlic, habanero pepper, salt, black pepper, and sausage; cook, stirring frequently, for 8 minutes longer.
- Now, pour in the eggs and sprinkle with thyme and marjoram; cook an additional 4 minutes, stirring with a spoon. Garnish with olives. Let cool completely.

Storing

Divide the sausage and eggs between two airtight containers. Refrigerate for up to 3 days.
For freezing, place each serving into individual plastic wrap and squeeze as much air as possible. Place them inside an airtight container and freeze up to 6 months.
Thaw the sausage and eggs before reheating in the microwave. Enjoy!

39. Curried Pickled Eggs

Ready in about 20 minutes
Servings 5

There are so many ways to eat eggs! Egg lovers will be absolutely delighted with this recipe!

Per serving: 145 Calories; 9g Fat; 2.8g Carbs; 11.4g Protein; 1.4g Sugars

Ingredients

10 eggs
1/2 cup onions, sliced
3 cardamom pods
1 tablespoon yellow curry powder
1 teaspoon yellow mustard seeds
2 clove garlic, sliced
1 cup cider vinegar
1 ¼ cups water
1 tablespoon salt

Directions

- Boil the eggs until hard-cooked; peel them and rinse under cold, running water. Add peeled eggs to a large-sized jar.
- Add all remaining ingredients to a pan that is preheated over a moderately high heat; bring to a rapid boil.
- Now, turn the heat to medium-low; let it simmer for 6 minutes. Let cool completely.

Storing

Spoon the chilled liquid into the jar. Keep in your refrigerator for 2 to 3 weeks. Bon appétit!

40. Italian-Style Egg and Mortadella Bites

Ready in about 5 minutes + chilling time
Servings 6

You will love this super-easy recipe. It features a few basic ingredients and takes under 5 minutes to make.

Per serving: 327 Calories; 25.7g Fat; 6.4g Carbs; 17g Protein; 1g Sugars

Ingredients

6 hard-boiled eggs, peeled and chopped
1/2 teaspoon Italian seasonings
1/3 cup mayonnaise
Sea salt and ground black pepper, to taste
1/2 teaspoon cayenne pepper
1/2 cup cream cheese, softened
6 slices Mortadella, chopped

Directions

- Combine all of the above ingredients in a mixing dish.
- Shape the mixture into balls.
- Transfer the balls to the refrigerator for 1 hour. Let cool completely.

Storing

Divide balls between three airtight containers or Ziploc bags; keep in your refrigerator for up 4 days.
For freezing, place balls in three airtight containers. Freeze up to 1 month. Defrost in the refrigerator. Bon appétit!

LUNCH

41. Broccoli and Baby Bella Mushrooms Delight

Ready in about 20 minutes
Servings 4

Broccoli is a powerhouse of many valuable nutrients. It fights cancer, boosts your immune system, and reduces many allergic reactions. Baby Bella mushrooms are a great source of vitamin B5, vitamin B3, copper, and selenium.

Per serving: 235 Calories; 20.9g Fat; 9.5g Carbs; 4.8g Protein; 2.7g Sugars

Ingredients

1/2 stick butter, room temperature
1/2 head broccoli, cut into small florets
10 ounces baby Bella mushrooms
1 teaspoon garlic, minced
1/3 cup chicken broth
1/3 cup whipping cream
1 teaspoon tarragon
1/2 teaspoon kosher salt, or more to taste
1/4 teaspoon crushed red pepper flakes
2 tablespoons Parmesan cheese
1/4 cup mayonnaise, preferably homemade

Directions

- Melt the butter in a skillet that is preheated over a moderate flame. Now, add the broccoli and mushrooms and cook until the mushrooms are slightly shriveled.
- Add the garlic and continue cooking until fragrant, stirring constantly.
- Add the broth, whipping cream and seasonings; cover with the lid and reduce the heat to medium-low. Cook an additional 10 minutes, stirring occasionally, until most of the liquid has evaporated.
- Stir the Parmesan cheese into the mushroom mixture until everything comes together. Let cool completely.

Storing

Divide the vegetables into four portions; divide the portions between four airtight containers; keep in your refrigerator for up 3 to 5 days.
For freezing, wrap them tightly with plastic wrap and place in airtight containers. Freeze up to 10 to 12 months. Defrost in the refrigerator. Bon appétit!

42. The Best Family Squash Stew

Ready in about 35 minutes
Servings 6

Vegetables are an extremely important part of every healthy diet, but when it comes to the keto diet, we find ourselves a bit confused. However, the more you learn about a keto diet, the more you know about combining food. For example, butternut squash contains 2.1 g carbs per 1 ounce.

Per serving: 113 Calories; 7.9g Fat; 9.7g Carbs; 2.8g Protein; 1.6g Sugars

Ingredients

1/2 stick butter
2 shallots, chopped
1 teaspoon garlic, finely chopped
6 ounces butternut squash, chopped
1 celery, chopped
2 tablespoons fresh cilantro, roughly chopped
1/2 teaspoon sea salt
1/4 teaspoon ground black pepper, or more to the taste
1/4 teaspoon smoked paprika, or more to the taste
1/2 teaspoon chili powder
1 pound ripe tomatoes, chopped
2 tablespoons red wine
1 bay leaf

Directions

- Melt the butter in a stock pot over a moderate heat. Now, sauté the shallots and garlic until fragrant, about 4 minutes.
- Add the eggplant, celery and cilantro; cook an additional 5 minutes.
- Stir in the remaining ingredients; reduce the heat to a medium-low and let it simmer, covered, for 20 to 25 minutes. Let cool completely.

Storing

Spoon the stew into three airtight containers; keep in your refrigerator for up to 3 to 4 days.
For freezing, place them in airtight containers or heavy-duty freezer bags. It will maintain the best quality for about 5 months. Defrost in the refrigerator. Enjoy!

43. Classic Creamy Cauliflower Soup

Ready in about 20 minutes
Servings 4

Is there anything better than a thick and creamy soup during winter weekdays? Serve warm with kale chips. So good, right?

Per serving: 260 Calories; 22.5g Fat; 11.1g Carbs; 7.2g Protein; 4.5g Sugars

Ingredients

3 cups chicken broth
3 cups cauliflower, cut into florets
1 cup almond milk, unsweetened
1 cup avocado, pitted and chopped
1/4 teaspoon Himalayan rock salt
1/4 teaspoon freshly cracked mixed peppercorns
1 bay leaf

Directions

- Simmer the chicken broth over a moderate flame. Add the cauliflower and cook for 10 minutes.
- Turn the heat to low. Add the remaining ingredients and cook for a further 5 minutes.
- Puree the mixture using an immersion blender. Let cool completely.

Storing

Spoon the soup into three airtight containers; keep in your refrigerator for up 3 to 4 days.
For freezing, place it in airtight containers or heavy-duty freezer bags. Freeze up to 4 to 6 months. Defrost in the microwave or refrigerator. Enjoy!

44. Rutabaga, Taro Leaf and Chicken Soup

Ready in about 45 minutes
Servings 4

You can use a small knife to test your chicken for doneness. If the juices run clear, the chicken is ready.

Per serving: 256 Calories; 8.9g Fat; 7.2g Carbs; 35.1g Protein; 3.4g Sugars

Ingredients

1 pound chicken thighs
1/2 cup rutabaga, cubed
2 carrots, peeled
2 celery stalks
1/2 cup leek, chopped
1/4 teaspoon garlic, granulated
1/4 teaspoon ground cloves
1/2 cup taro leaves, roughly chopped
1 tablespoon fresh parsley, chopped
Salt and black pepper, to taste
1 cup chicken consommé, canned
3 cups water
1 teaspoon cayenne pepper

Directions

- Add all of the above ingredients, except for cayenne pepper, to a large-sized stock pot. Bring to a rapid boil over high heat.
- Now, turn the heat to medium-low. Let it simmer, partially covered, an additional 35 minutes or until the chicken is pinkish-brown.
- Next, discard the chicken and vegetables. Add cayenne pepper to the broth; allow it to simmer an additional 8 minutes.
- When the chicken thighs are cool enough to handle, cut off the meat from bones. Afterwards, add the meat back to the soup. Let cool completely.

Storing

Spoon the soup into three airtight containers; keep in your refrigerator for up 3 to 4 days.
For freezing, spoon it into airtight containers or heavy-duty freezer bags. Freeze up to 4 to 6 months. Defrost in the microwave or refrigerator. Enjoy!

45. Sensational Chicken Wings with Broccoli

Ready in about 50 minutes
Servings 4

Finger-lickin' chicken wings can be made right at home with this surprisingly simple recipe. Cruciferous vegetable like broccoli pairs perfectly with crispy chicken wings.

Per serving: 450 Calories; 35.5g Fat; 9.6g Carbs; 25.1g Protein; 2.8g Sugars

Ingredients

1 pound chicken wings
1 pound broccoli, broken into florets
1 carrot, sliced
1 cup scallions, chopped
1 teaspoon garlic paste
1 teaspoon Italian seasoning mix (such as Old Sub Sailor)
3 tablespoons olive oil
2 cups Colby cheese, shredded

Directions

- Preheat your oven to 390 degrees F. Lightly grease a rimmed baking sheet.
- Roast the wings until cooked through and skin is crispy, about 35 minutes. Add broccoli, carrots, scallions, and garlic paste.
- Season the chicken and broccoli with Italian seasoning mix; drizzle them with olive oil.
- Roast an additional 13 to 15 minutes. Scatter shredded cheese over the top. Let cool completely.

Storing

Place chicken wings in airtight containers or Ziploc bags; keep in your refrigerator for up 3 to 4 days.
For freezing, place them in airtight containers or heavy-duty freezer bags. Freeze up to 3 months. Once thawed in the refrigerator, heat in the preheated oven at 375 degrees F for 20 to 25 minutes or until heated through. Enjoy!

46. Eggplant and Duck Quiche

Ready in about 45 minutes
Servings 4

Ground duck meat has a great texture like beef and an exceptional taste and nutritional benefits like chicken. Serve at room temperature.

Per serving: 562 Calories; 49.5g Fat; 6.7g Carbs; 22.5g Protein; 2.4g Sugars

Ingredients

1 ½ cups almond flour
1/2 teaspoon kosher salt
8 eggs
1 ½ tablespoons butter, melted
1 pound ground duck meat
1/4 teaspoon ground black pepper
1/2 teaspoon celery seeds
1/2 teaspoon basil, dried
1/3 cup whipping cream
1/2 pound eggplant, peeled and sliced

Directions

- Preheat your oven to 350 degrees F
- Mix almond flour with kosher salt. Fold in an egg and melted butter; mix to combine well.
- Now, press the crust into the bottom of a lightly-greased baking dish.
- Then, heat up a skillet and brown ground duck meat for 2 to 3 minutes, stirring continuously.
- In a mixing bowl, combine the remaining eggs with black pepper, celery seeds, basil, and whipping cream.
- Stir in browned meat; stir until everything is thoroughly combined. Pour the mixture into the prepared crust. Add the eggplant slices.
- Bake your quiche for 37 to 42 minutes. Transfer to a wire rack to cool before slicing.

Storing

Slice the quiche into four pieces; divide between airtight containers or Ziploc bags; keep in your refrigerator for up to 3 days.
For freezing, place them in airtight containers or heavy-duty freezer bags. Freeze up to 3 months. Once thawed in the refrigerator, heat in the microwave until warmed through. Enjoy!

47. Mediterranean Chicken Legs in Sauce

Ready in about 50 minutes
Servings 6

Doubtless, with this recipe, you can bring Mediterranean aroma and flavor into your own kitchen. This chicken recipe might become a big hit in your home!

Per serving: 333 Calories; 20.2g Fat; 2g Carbs; 33.5g Protein; 0.3g Sugars

Ingredients

2 tablespoons ghee
1 ½ pounds chicken legs, skinless
1/2 cup scallions, chopped
2 garlic cloves, minced
1/2 cup dry sherry
1 rosemary sprig, chopped
2 thyme sprigs, chopped
1 tablespoon fresh oregano, chopped
1 tablespoon fresh basil, chopped
1 cup heavy cream
1/2 teaspoon salt
1/2 teaspoon mixed peppercorns, freshly crushed

Directions

- Preheat your oven to 400 degrees F.
- Melt the ghee in a pan that is preheated over a moderate flame; now, brown the chicken legs for 6 to 8 minutes.
- After that, stir in the scallions, garlic, sherry, and herbs. Transfer to a lightly greased casserole dish and cover it.
- Bake for 35 minutes or until a meat thermometer registers 165 degrees F; reserve.
- Mix cooking juices with heavy cream, salt and crushed peppercorns; simmer for a couple of minutes or until it is thickened and cooked through.

Storing

Place chicken legs along with sauce in airtight containers or Ziploc bags; keep in your refrigerator for up to 3 to 4 days.
For freezing, place them in airtight containers or heavy-duty freezer bags. Freeze up to 3 months. Once thawed in the refrigerator, heat in the preheated oven at 375 degrees F for 20 to 25 minutes. Bon appétit!

48. The Easiest Meatballs Ever

Ready in about 30 minutes
Servings 6

If you are a great believer in a combination of simplicity and tradition, this recipe will be perfect for you! It is important to place your meatballs under the broiler. Otherwise, they turn mushy and pretty tasteless.

Per serving: 284 Calories; 14.8g Fat; 1.3g Carbs; 34.4g Protein; 0.3g Sugars

Ingredients

For the Meatballs:
1 pound ground pork
1/2 pound ground beef
1 tablespoon beef bouillon granules
2 small-sized eggs
2 cloves garlic, minced
1 tablespoon Montreal steak seasoning

For the Sauce:
3 teaspoons butter
1/2 teaspoon dried thyme
Salt and pepper to taste
1 cup bone broth
1 cup heavy whipping cream
Salt and pepper, to taste

Directions

- Begin by preheating an oven to 360 degrees F.
- Thoroughly combine all ingredients for the meatballs in a mixing bowl. Shape into 20 balls with oiled hands.
- Arrange the meatballs on a cookie sheet that is previously greased with a nonstick cooking spray.
- Bake for 18 to 22 minutes or until the meatballs are thoroughly cooked. Now, place your meatballs under the broiler for a couple of minutes to achieve a browned, crispy crust.
- Meanwhile, make the sauce in a pan. Firstly, melt the butter over a moderate heat. Slowly and gradually stir in the other ingredients for the sauce, whisking constantly.
- Bring to a boil and cook until the sauce is thickened.

Storing

Place meatballs along with the sauce in airtight containers or Ziploc bags; keep in your refrigerator for up to 3 to 4 days.
Freeze the meatballs in the sauce in airtight containers or heavy-duty freezer bags. Freeze up to 3 to 4 months. To defrost, slowly reheat in a saucepan. Bon appétit!

49. Oven-Roasted Pork Cutlets with Veggies

Ready in about 30 minutes + marinating time
Servings 4

On a bed of roasted veggies, pork cutlets are even more delicious! You can use another combo of low-carb vegetables if desired.

Per serving: 452 Calories; 34.8g Fat; 6.7g Carbs; 26.3g Protein; 2.5g Sugars

Ingredients

1 teaspoon garlic paste
1/2 teaspoon sea salt
1/2 teaspoon freshly ground black pepper
1 tablespoon yellow mustard
2 tablespoons cider vinegar
2 tablespoons lard, melted
4 pork cutlets
1 celery stalk, diced
2 carrots, sliced
1 cup leeks, sliced

Directions

- In a mixing bowl, combine the garlic paste, salt, black pepper, mustard and cider vinegar until well mixed. Add the pork cutlets and let them marinate for 2 hours.
- Now, melt the lard in an oven-safe pan over a moderate heat. Brown pork cutlets for 5 minutes on each side. Add the celery, carrots, and leeks.
- Cook an additional 5 minutes, stirring periodically.
- Transfer the pan to the oven; roast the pork with vegetables about 13 minutes. Let cool completely.

Storing

Divide pork cutlets and veggies into four portions; place each portion in a separate airtight container or Ziploc bag; keep in your refrigerator for 3 to 4 days. Freeze the pork cutlets and veggies in airtight containers or heavy-duty freezer bags. Freeze up to 4 months.
Remove the pork cutlets and veggies from the freezer and place them in the refrigerator. Reheat the pork cutlets in the same way you prepared them, if possible.

50. The Best Sloppy Joes Ever

Ready in about 30 minutes
Servings 6

Make sure to choose a chuck with a good fat content; otherwise, your Sloppy Joes will come out dry.

Per serving: 313 Calories; 20.6g Fat; 3.5g Carbs; 26.6g Protein; 0.3g Sugars

Ingredients

2 teaspoons tallow, room temperature
2 shallots, finely chopped
1 teaspoon garlic, minced
1 ½ pounds ground chuck
1/2 cup pureed tomatoes
1 teaspoon deli mustard
1 teaspoon celery seeds
1 tablespoon coconut vinegar
Salt and ground pepper, to taste
1 teaspoon cayenne pepper
1 teaspoon chipotle powder

Directions

- Melt 1 tablespoons of tallow in a heavy-bottomed skillet over a moderately high flame.
- Now, sauté the shallots and garlic until tender and aromatic; reserve.
- In the same skillet, melt another tablespoon of tallow. Now, brown ground chuck, crumbling with a spatula.
- Add the vegetables back to the skillet; stir in the remaining ingredients. Turn the heat to medium-low; simmer for 20 minutes, stirring periodically. Let cool completely.

Storing

Place the meat mixture in airtight containers or Ziploc bags; keep in your refrigerator for up to 3 to 4 days. For freezing, place the meat mixture in airtight containers or heavy-duty freezer bags. Freeze up to 2 to 3 months. Defrost in the refrigerator. Bon appétit!

51. Grilled Rib Eye Steak

Ready in about 20 minutes
Servings 6

Use a meat thermometer to determine the level of doneness of the meat. Here are the temperatures: Rare = 120 degrees F; Medium rare = 130 degrees F; Medium = 140 degrees F; Well-done = 160 degrees F.

Per serving: 314 Calories; 11.4g Fat; 1g Carbs; 48.2g Protein; 0.6g Sugars

Ingredients

1 tablespoon oyster sauce
1 tablespoon Worcestershire sauce
2 tablespoons Swerve sweetener
2 garlic cloves, smashed
1 thyme sprig, chopped
2 rosemary sprigs, chopped
1 teaspoon dried sage, crushed
1/2 teaspoon chipotle powder
Celery salt and ground black pepper, to taste
2 tablespoons dry red wine
2 tablespoons olive oil
2 pounds rib eye steaks

Directions

- In a mixing bowl, thoroughly combine oyster sauce, Worcestershire sauce, Swerve, garlic, thyme, rosemary, sage, chipotle powder, salt, pepper, wine and olive oil.
- Now, marinate the rib eye steaks in your refrigerator overnight.
- Preheat your grill that is previously lightly greased. Grill rib eye steaks over direct heat for 4 to 5 minutes on each side for medium-rare. Let cool completely.

Storing

Divide the rib eye steaks between three airtight containers or Ziploc bags; keep in your refrigerator for 3 to 4 days.
For freezing, place the rib eye steaks in airtight containers or heavy-duty freezer bags. Freeze up to 3 months. Defrost in the refrigerator. Bon appétit!

52. Winter Guinness Beef Stew

Ready in about 1 hour
Servings 6

This Irish-style stew will blow your mind! Don't forget about browning meat, it will add an excellent flavor to this stew. You can add a hot pepper sauce if your family likes a spicy food!

Per serving: 444 Calories; 14.2g Fat; 7.1g Carbs; 66.3g Protein; 2.7g Sugars

Ingredients

1 ½ tablespoons canola oil
1 ½ pounds chuck shoulder, cut into bite-size cubes
1 cup leeks, chopped
1 celery stalk, chopped
1 parsnip, chopped
2 carrots, chopped
1 ½ cups tomato puree
3 cups boiling water
1 cup Guinness beer
1 tablespoon beef bouillon granules
1 bay leaf
1/2 teaspoon caraway seeds
1/4 cup mint leaves, chopped, to serve

Directions

- Heat the oil in a stockpot over medium-high heat. Now, sauté chuck shoulder cubes until they are browned; reserve.
- Then, sauté the vegetables in pan drippings for 8 minutes, stirring periodically.
- Throw in the remaining ingredients, except for mint leaves, and bring to a rapid boil. Now, turn the heat to medium-low; let it simmer about 50 minutes; garnished with mint leaves. Let cool completely.

Storing

Spoon the stew into three airtight containers; keep in your refrigerator for 3 to 4 days.
For freezing, place the stew in heavy-duty freezer bags. When the bags are frozen through, stack them up like file folders to save space in the freezer. Freeze up to 4 months.
Defrost in the microwave or refrigerator. Enjoy!

53. Stuffed Tomatoes with Cotija Cheese

Ready in about 35 minutes
Servings 4

Make these amazing stuffed tomatoes and you won't miss a bun. All the comfort without any guilt.

Per serving: 244 Calories; 9.6g Fat; 11g Carbs; 28.9g Protein; 7g Sugars

Ingredients

1 tablespoon olive oil
1 cup scallions, chopped
2 cloves garlic, minced
1 pound ground beef
2 tablespoons tomato paste, sugar-free
Salt and pepper, to your liking
1/2 teaspoon cumin seeds
8 tomatoes, scoop out the pulp and chop it
1 teaspoon mild paprika
1 teaspoon dried coriander leaves
1/2 cup beef broth
3/4 cup Cotija cheese, shredded

Directions

- Start by preheating your oven to 350 degrees F. Lightly grease a casserole dish with a cooking spray.
- Heat the oil in a saucepan over a moderately high heat. Sauté the scallions and garlic until aromatic.
- Stir in ground meat; cook for 5 minutes, crumbling with a spatula. Add tomato paste and cook until heated through. Season with salt, pepper and cumin seeds.
- Fill the tomatoes with beef mixture and transfer them to the prepared casserole dish.
- In a mixing bowl, whisk tomato pulp with paprika, coriander and broth. Pour the mixture over the stuffed tomatoes.
- Bake until tomatoes are tender, about 20 minutes. Top with Cotija cheese and bake an additional 5 minutes. Let cool completely.

Storing

Place stuffed tomatoes in airtight containers or Ziploc bags; keep in your refrigerator for 3 to 4 days.
Wrap each stuffed tomato tightly in several layers of plastic wrap and squeeze the air out. Place them in a freezable container; they can be frozen for up to 1 month. Bake the thawed stuffed tomatoes in your oven at 200 degrees F until they are completely warm.

54. Smoky and Yummy Beef Medley

Ready in about 1 hour 40 minutes
Servings 6

Cook beef sirloin steak until meltingly tender in spicy juices. Serve with a dollop of full-fat sour cream.

Per serving: 375 Calories; 13.3g Fat; 5.6g Carbs; 55.1g Protein; 2.9g Sugars

Ingredients

3 teaspoons tallow, room temperature
2 pounds boneless beef sirloin steak, cubed
Seasoned salt and cayenne pepper, to taste
1/2 teaspoon black peppercorns, crushed
1 cup yellow onions, chopped
2 cloves garlic, minced
1 tablespoon smoked paprika
1 teaspoon caraway seeds, crushed
1/2 teaspoon mustard seeds
2 thyme sprigs
1 rosemary sprig
6 cups bone broth
1 tablespoon fish sauce
2 ripe Roma tomatoes, pureed
1 tablespoon dry white wine
2 bay leaves

Directions

- Heat 1 teaspoon of tallow in a heavy-bottomed pot over a moderate heat. Now, brown the beef until it is no longer pink.
- Season with salt, cayenne pepper, and black peppercorns; reserve.
- In the same pot, heat remaining 2 teaspoons of tallow over a moderate heat. Cook the onions and garlic until they're softened, stirring continuously.
- Now, add the paprika, caraway seeds, mustard seeds, thyme, and rosemary; cook an additional minute or until they are fragrant.
- Add the remaining ingredients. Cook, partially covered, for 1 hour 30 minutes more. Discard bay leaves. Let cool completely.

Storing

Spoon the medley into three airtight containers; keep in your refrigerator for 3 to 4 days.
For freezing, place the medley in airtight containers or heavy-duty freezer bags. Freeze up to 4 months. Defrost in the microwave. Bon appétit!

55. Beef Soup with Chili Drizzle

Ready in about 1 hour 10 minutes
Servings 6

This rich and flavorful soup highlights the sweet flavor of green peas as well as the spiciness of chili drizzle. Chopped fresh cilantro works well too.

Per serving: 375 Calories; 14.4g Fat; 11.8g Carbs; 47.6g Protein; 4.7g Sugars

Ingredients

1 tablespoon canola oil
2 pounds beef chuck (well-marbled), boneless and cubed
2 onions, peeled and chopped
1 parsnip, chopped
1 celery with leaves, chopped
2 carrots, chopped
1/2 cup ripe olives, pitted and halved
1 ripe tomato, pureed
6 cups water
2 tablespoons instant bouillon granules
1/2 teaspoon ground bay leaf
1/2 teaspoon ground cumin
1/2 cup frozen green peas

For the chili drizzle:
2 red chilies
1 tablespoon extra-virgin olive oil
2 tablespoons lemon juice
Salt, to taste

Directions

- Heat the oil in a stockpot over a moderately high heat. Now, brown the beef cubes for 3 to 5 minutes, stirring often; reserve.
- Next, in pan drippings, cook the onions, parsnip, celery and carrots until just tender. Add the olives, tomato, water, bouillon granules, ground bay leaf and cumin.
- Stir in reserved beef and bring the soup to a boil.
- Turn the heat to medium-low; let it simmer, partially covered, about 50 minutes. Add green peas and cook for a further 15 minutes.
- Meanwhile, make the chili drizzle by blending all ingredients in your food processor. Afterwards, top with chili drizzle. Let cool completely.

Storing

Spoon the soup into three airtight containers; keep in your refrigerator for up to 4 days.
For freezing, place the soup in airtight containers or heavy-duty freezer bags. Freeze up to 4 to 6 months. Defrost in the microwave or refrigerator. Bon appétit!

56. Hot and Spicy Fish Stew

Ready in about 25 minutes
Servings 4

This is an easy and versatile fish stew recipe. You can experiment with ingredients, from fish and seafood to seasonings and wine. Shrimp, scallops, and salmon work well too.

Per serving: 296 Calories; 8.6g Fat; 5.5g Carbs; 41.4g Protein; 2.7g Sugars

Ingredients

1 tablespoon sesame oil
1 cup onions, chopped
1 teaspoon garlic, smashed
Sea salt, to taste
4 cups water
1 cup fresh tomato, pureed
1 tablespoon chicken bouillon granules
1/2 pound sea bass, cut into 2-inch pieces
1/3 pound halibut, cut into 2-inch pieces
2 rosemary sprigs, chopped
1/2 cup Sauvignon blanc
1/8 teaspoon Tabasco sauce, or more to taste

Directions

- Heat the oil in a large stockpot that is preheated over medium heat. Now, sauté the onions and garlic until they're softened and aromatic.
- Add the salt, water, tomato and chicken bouillon granules; cook an additional 13 minutes.
- Stir in the remaining ingredients and bring to a rolling boil.
- After that, turn the heat to medium-low and let it simmer until the fish easily flakes apart, about 4 minutes.
- Taste and adjust the seasonings. Let cool completely.

Storing

Spoon fish stew into three airtight containers; it will last for 3 to 4 days in the refrigerator.
For freezing, place fish stew in airtight containers or heavy-duty freezer bags. Freeze up to 4 to 6 months. Defrost in the microwave or refrigerator. Bon appétit!

57. Easy Oven-Baked Cod Fillets

Ready in about 30 minutes
Servings 4

Cod is a great source of protein, omega-3 fatty acids, and vitamin B12. Did you know that cod liver oil could lower your blood pressure, prevent heart disease, and protect eyesight?

Per serving: 195 Calories; 8.2g Fat; 0.5g Carbs; 28.7g Protein; 0.1g Sugars

Ingredients

2 tablespoons olive oil
1/2 tablespoon yellow mustard
1 teaspoon garlic paste
1/2 tablespoon fresh lemon juice
1/2 teaspoon shallot powder
Salt and ground black pepper, to taste
1/2 teaspoon red pepper flakes, crushed
4 cod fillets
1/4 cup fresh cilantro, chopped

Directions

- Start by preheating your oven to 420 degrees F. Lightly grease a baking dish with a nonstick cooking spray.
- In a small mixing dish, thoroughly combine the oil, mustard, garlic paste, lemon juice, shallot powder, salt, black pepper and red pepper.
- Rub this mixture on all sides of your fish.
- Bake 15 to 22 minutes in the middle of the preheated oven. Garnish with fresh cilantro. Let cool completely.

Storing

Place cod fillets in airtight containers; it will last for 3 to 4 days in the refrigerator.
For freezing, place cod fillets in airtight containers or heavy-duty freezer bags. Freeze up to 2 to 3 months. Defrost in the refrigerator. Bon appétit!

58. Sriracha and Scallion Chuck

Ready in about 50 minutes
Servings 4

This isn't an average recipe for chuck pot roast. This chuck is marinated in Sriracha-scallion sauce and then, cooked to perfection in hot tallow.

Per serving: 292 Calories; 14.3g Fat; 3.9g Carbs; 36.9g Protein; 1.7g Sugars

Ingredients

2 tablespoons soy sauce
1 teaspoon Sriracha sauce
1 tablespoon garlic paste
Salt and crushed mixed peppercorns, to taste
1 teaspoon mustard seeds
1/2 teaspoon dried marjoram
1 bunch scallions, chopped
1/2 tablespoon tallow
1 ½ pounds chuck pot roast, cubed
1/4 teaspoon cumin
1/4 teaspoon celery seeds
1 tablespoon fresh parsley, roughly chopped

Directions

- Whisk the soy sauce, Sriracha sauce and garlic paste in a mixing bowl. Add the salt, crushed peppercorns, mustard seeds, marjoram, and scallions.
- Add the cubed beef and let it marinate for 40 minutes in your refrigerator.
- Melt the tallow a frying pan over a moderately high heat. Cook marinated beef for 5 to 6 minutes, stirring frequently; work in batches to cook beef cubes through evenly.
- Season with cumin and celery seeds. Garnish with fresh parsley. Let cool completely.

Storing

Divide the meat between four airtight containers or Ziploc bags; keep in your refrigerator for up 3 to 4 days.
For freezing, place the meat in airtight containers or heavy-duty freezer bags. Freeze up to 2 to 3 months. Defrost in the refrigerator. Enjoy!

59. Hungarian Beef Stew

Ready in about 1 hour 25 minutes
Servings 4

Here is an ideal recipe for cheap cuts! A traditional Hungarian stew highlights the best of their amazingly rich and delicious cuisine.

Per serving: 357 Calories; 15.8g Fat; 10g Carbs; 40.2g Protein; 4.2g Sugars

Ingredients

2 tablespoons olive oil
1 ¼ pounds chuck-eye roast, diced
Celery salt and ground black pepper, to taste
1 tablespoon Hungarian paprika
1 tablespoon pear cider vinegar
1/2 cup Cabernet Sauvignon
4 cups water
2 tablespoons beef bouillon granules
1/4 teaspoon ground bay leaf
2 onions, peeled and chopped
1 celery with leaves, chopped
2 carrots, peeled and cut into 1/4-inch rounds
1 tablespoon flaxseed meal

Directions

- Heat the oil in a heavy-bottomed pot. Then, cook the meat until no longer pink, for 3 to 4 minutes; work in batches and set aside. Season with celery salt, pepper, and Hungarian paprika.
- Now, pour the vinegar and Cabernet Sauvignon to deglaze the bottom of the pot. Add the water, beef bouillon granules and reserved beef to the pot.
- Stir in the ground bay leaf, onions, celery and carrots and cook an additional 1 hour 15 minutes over medium-low heat.
- Add the flaxseed meal to thicken the liquid; stir constantly for 3 minutes. Let cool completely.

Storing

Spoon the stew into four airtight containers; keep in your refrigerator for up to 4 days.
For freezing, place the stew in airtight containers or heavy-duty freezer bags. Freeze up to 4 to 6 months. Defrost in the microwave or refrigerator. Bon appétit!

60. Spicy Pork Sausage Frittata

Ready in about 35 minutes
Servings 4

This recipe is so versatile so you can try a different keto breakfast every morning! Combine the eggs with a pork sausage, ham, bacon, prosciutto or ground meat.

Per serving: 423 Calories; 35.4g Fat; 4.1g Carbs; 22.6g Protein; 2g Sugars

Ingredients

3 tablespoons olive oil
1 cup onion, chopped
1 teaspoon jalapeno pepper, finely minced
2 garlic cloves, minced
1 teaspoon salt
1/2 teaspoon ground black pepper
1/4 teaspoon cayenne pepper
1/2 pound pork sausages, thinly sliced
8 eggs, beaten
1 teaspoon dried sage, crushed

Directions

- Heat the oil in a nonstick skillet over a medium-high heat. Now, sauté the onions, peppers and garlic until the onion becomes translucent, about 4 minutes.
- Season with salt, black pepper, and cayenne pepper. Then, stir in the sausage and cook, stirring often, until they're no longer pink.
- Transfer the mixture to a lightly greased baking dish. Pour the eggs over the top and sprinkle with dried sage.
- Bake in the preheated oven at 420 degrees F for 25 minutes. Let cool completely.

Storing

Cut the frittata into four wedges. Place each of them in an airtight container; place in the refrigerator for 3 to 4 days.
To freeze, place in separate Ziploc bags and freeze up to 3 months. To defrost, place in your microwave for a few minutes.

61. Colorful Vegetable and Broccoli Rice

Ready in about 20 minutes
Servings 4

If you can make cauli rice, you should try broccoli rice. Use a food processor or box grater for this purpose. Add some colorful veggies and enjoy!

Per serving: 126 Calories; 11.6g Fat; 5.4g Carbs; 1.3g Protein; 2.5g Sugars

Ingredients

1 head broccoli, broken into florets
1/2 stick butter
1/2 yellow onion, chopped
1 garlic clove, minced
1 red bell pepper, chopped
1 Aji Fantasy chili pepper, minced
1/2 celery stalk, chopped
Salt and ground black pepper, to taste

Directions

- Blitz the broccoli in your food processor until it has reached a rice-like texture.
- Now, melt the butter in a sauté pan over a moderate heat. Sweat yellow onion for 2 to 3 minutes; stir in the garlic and cook until slightly browned and fragrant.
- After that, add the peppers and celery; cook an additional 4 minutes or until they're just tender. Add broccoli "rice" and season with salt and pepper.
- Cook for a further 5 minutes, stirring periodically. Let cool completely.

Storing

Spoon the broccoli rice into four airtight containers; keep in your refrigerator for 3 to 5 days.
For freezing, place the broccoli rice in airtight containers or heavy-duty freezer bags. Freeze up to 10 to 12 months. Defrost in the microwave. Bon appétit!

62. Sour Cream Cabbage Soup

Ready in about 25 minutes
Servings 4

You won't be able to resist this hearty soup that is sure to please. Make sure to use full-fat sour cream in this recipe.

Per serving: 185 Calories; 16.6g Fat; 7.4g Carbs; 2.9g Protein; 2.1g Sugars

Ingredients

1 ½ tablespoons butter, melted
1 leek, chopped
2 garlic cloves, minced
2 carrots, chopped
1 cup cabbage, shredded
1 green pepper, chopped
4 cups water
2 bouillon cubes
1 cup sour cream
Fresh tarragon sprigs, for garnish

Directions

- Warm the butter in a large pot over medium flame. Sauté the leeks until just tender and fragrant. Now, add the remaining vegetables and cook for 5 to 7 minutes, stirring periodically.
- Add the water and bouillon cubes; cover partially and cook an additional 13 minutes.
- Blend the mixture until creamy, uniform and smooth. Stir in the sour cream; gently heat, stirring continuously, until your soup is hot.
- Garnish with fresh tarragon. Let cool completely.

Storing

Spoon the soup into four airtight containers; keep in your refrigerator for up to 4 days.
For freezing, place the soup in heavy-duty freezer bags. When the bags are frozen through, stack them up like file folders to save space in the freezer.
Freeze up to 4 months. Defrost in the microwave or refrigerator. Bon appétit!

63. The Best Ever Chicken Stew

Ready in about 1 hour
Servings 6

Winter is the perfect time of the year to enjoy a hearty and spicy chicken stew. These simply chicken drumsticks, gently cooked with beautiful vegetables and aromatics, are guaranteed to hit the spot!

Per serving: 239 Calories; 9.7g Fat; 11.5g Carbs; 25.6g Protein; 4.9g Sugars

Ingredients

2 tablespoons tallow, room temperature
2 medium-sized shallots, finely chopped
2 garlic cloves, sliced
1 quart chicken broth
1 sprig rosemary
1 teaspoon dried marjoram
1 pound chicken drumsticks
1 celery, chopped
1/2 pound carrots, chopped
1 bell pepper, chopped
1 poblano pepper, chopped
2 ripe tomatoes, chopped
1 teaspoon salt
1/2 teaspoon ground black pepper
1/2 teaspoon smoked paprika

Directions

- Melt the tallow in a large heavy pot that is preheated over a moderate flame. Sweat the shallots and garlic until aromatic and just tender.
- Now, turn the heat to medium-high. Stir in the chicken broth, rosemary, marjoram, and chicken drumsticks; bring to a boil.
- Add the remaining ingredients and reduce the heat to medium-low. Simmer, covered, for 50 minutes.
- Discard the bones and chop the chicken into small chunks. Let cool completely.

Storing

Spoon the stew into three airtight containers; keep in your refrigerator for 3 to 4 days.
For freezing, place the stew in airtight containers or heavy-duty freezer bags. It will maintain the best quality for about 4 to 6 months. Defrost in the microwave or refrigerator. Bon appétit!

64. Country Chicken Soup with Root Vegetables

Ready in about 25 minutes
Servings 4

Cozy up to a bowl of a delicious chicken soup this autumn. This rustic soup can be blended to give a smooth texture, if desired.

Per serving: 342 Calories; 22.4g Fat; 10.3g Carbs; 25.2g Protein; 5.4g Sugars

Ingredients

1 tablespoon olive oil
1 teaspoon garlic, finely minced
1 parsnip, chopped
1/2 cup turnip, chopped
1 carrot, chopped
2 chicken breasts, boneless and cut into chunks
Salt and pepper, to taste
4 cups water
1 cup full-fat milk
1 cup heavy cream
2 bouillon cubes
1 whole egg
4 tablespoons fresh chives, roughly chopped

Directions

- Heat the oil in a heavy pot over a moderate heat; now, cook the garlic until aromatic. Add the parsnip, turnip and carrot. Cook until your vegetables are softened.
- Stir in the chicken; cook until it is no longer pink, for 3 to 4 minutes, stirring periodically. Season with salt and pepper.
- Pour in the water, milk, and heavy cream. Add the bouillon cubes and bring it to a boil.
- Reduce the heat to medium-low; let it simmer for 20 minutes longer. Add the beaten egg and stir an additional minute.
- Remove from the heat; garnish with chopped chives. Let cool completely.

Storing

Spoon the soup into four airtight containers or Ziploc bags; keep in your refrigerator for up to 3 to 4 days.
For freezing, place the stew in airtight containers. It will maintain the best quality for about 4 to 6 months. Defrost in the refrigerator. Bon appétit!

65. Mushroom and Caciocavallo Stuffed Peppers

Ready in about 30 minutes
Servings 6

These simple but endlessly crave-worthy peppers are both elegant and rustic. The secret lies in the simple approach - fresh button mushrooms, tomato sauce and mellow Caciocavallo cheese.

Per serving: 319 Calories; 8.8g Fat; 5.6g Carbs; 10.3g Protein; 8.5g Sugars

Ingredients

2 tablespoons avocado oil
1 shallot, chopped
1 teaspoon garlic, minced
3/4 pound button mushrooms, chopped
1 teaspoon Pimento
2 tablespoons fresh chives, chopped
1 teaspoon caraway seeds
Salt to taste
6 bell peppers, seeds and tops removed
1/2 cup Caciocavallo cheese, grated
1/2 cup tomato sauce

Directions

- Preheat your oven to 380 degrees F. Heat the oil in a pan that is preheated over moderately high heat.
- Sauté the shallots and garlic until the shallot softens. Stir in the mushrooms and cook an additional 4 minutes or until the mushrooms are fragrant.
- Add pimento, chives, caraway seeds and salt; stir until everything is heated through.
- Place the peppers in a foil-lined roasting pan; fill them with the mushroom stuffing. Top each pepper with Caciocavallo cheese.
- Afterwards, pour the tomato sauce over everything. Bake for 18 to 23 minutes or until cheese is lightly browned. Let cool completely.

Storing

Place stuffed peppers in airtight containers; keep in your refrigerator for 3 to 4 days.
Wrap each stuffed pepper tightly in several layers of plastic wrap and squeeze the air out. Place them in airtight containers; they can be frozen for up to 1 month. Bake the thawed stuffed peppers at 200 degrees F until they are completely warm.

66. Hungarian-Style Chicken Fillets

Ready in about 30 minutes
Servings 6

Hungarian cuisine is well known for its spices such as paprika, which give taste, color and heat to any traditional dish. In this recipe, caraway seeds and lemon rind work well too.

Per serving: 239 Calories; 8.6g Fat; 5.5g Carbs; 34.3g Protein; 3.3g Sugars

Ingredients

1 ½ pounds chicken fillets
1 teaspoon garlic paste
1 teaspoon Hungarian paprika
1/2 teaspoon marjoram
1 teaspoon dry thyme
1 teaspoon coarse salt
1/2 teaspoon freshly ground black pepper
1/2 cup tomato sauce, preferably homemade
1/4 cup low-sodium soy sauce
1 bell pepper, deveined and chopped
1 large-sized red onion, chopped
2 tablespoons curly parsley, for garnish

Directions

- Rub each chicken fillet with the garlic paste and seasonings. Place in a heavy pot that is preheated over medium flame.
- Cook for 4 to 5 minutes on each side.
- Pour in tomato sauce and soy sauce; bring it to a boil. Add bell pepper and onion.
- Reduce the heat to medium-low. Cook, partially covered, for 25 minutes more; garnish with fresh parsley. Let cool completely.

Storing

Place chicken fillets in airtight containers or Ziploc bags; keep in your refrigerator for up to 3 to 4 days. For freezing, place them in airtight containers or heavy-duty freezer bags. Freeze up to 4 months. Once thawed in the refrigerator, reheat them in a saucepan. Bon appétit!

67. Top Round Steak with Marsala Sauce

Ready in about 1 hour 40 minutes
Servings 4

You can substitute top round steak with top sirloin in this recipe. Bear in mind that top round contains less fat than top sirloin which means you should use a liquid throughout the cooking process.

Per serving: 339 Calories; 21.7g Fat; 9.2g Carbs; 35g Protein; 1.2g Sugars

Ingredients

1 ½ pounds top round steak, cut into 4 serving-size pieces
2 tablespoons olive oil
1 shallot, chopped
1 garlic clove, pressed
1 ½ cups Brussels sprouts, quartered
1 teaspoon ground bay leaf
1/2 teaspoon dried basil
1 tablespoon dried sage, crushed
1/2 teaspoon sea salt
1/4 teaspoon freshly ground black pepper
1 cup broth

For the Sauce:
1/2 cup Marsala wine
1/2 cup chicken broth
1/4 teaspoon freshly grated nutmeg
3/4 teaspoon Dijon mustard
1 cup double cream

Directions

- Begin by preheating your oven to 340 degrees F. Flatten each top round steak with a meat tenderizer.
- Heat olive oil in an oven-safe pan over medium-high heat. Now, cook the steak until just browned; reserve.
- Next, cook the shallots and garlic in pan drippings in the same pan until they're softened. After that, cook Brussels sprouts until tender and smell good.
- Add the round steak back to the pan. Season with ground bay leaf, basil, sage, salt, and pepper. Pour in 1 cup of broth. Wrap with foil and roast for 1 hour 10 minutes.
- Add the wine, 1/2 cup chicken cup of broth and nutmeg to the same roasting pan. Let it simmer for 15 to 18 minutes or until the sauce is reduced to half.
- Now, stir in the mustard and double cream; cook an additional 15 minutes or until everything is heated through. Let cool completely.

Storing

Divide the steaks between four airtight containers or Ziploc bags; keep in your refrigerator for up to 3 to 4 days. Place Marsala sauce in an airtight container and keep in your refrigerator for up to 4 days. For freezing, place the steaks in airtight containers or heavy-duty freezer bags. Freeze up to 3 months. Defrost in the refrigerator. Bon appétit!

68. Buttery Roasted Chuck with Horseradish Sauce

Ready in about 2 hours
Servings 6

Check out this buttery-tender chuck that is marinated with dry red wine, mustard, and fragrant Italian seasoning mix.

Per serving: 493 Calories; 39.4g Fat; 2.9g Carbs; 27.9g Protein; 0.8g Sugars

Ingredients

1 ½ pounds chuck
2 bay leaves
1/4 cup vegetable oil
1 garlic clove, minced
1 tablespoon Italian seasoning mix
1 ½ tablespoons whole grain mustard
1/3 cup dry red wine
1 teaspoon sea salt
1/4 teaspoon black pepper, to taste
1/2 teaspoon cayenne pepper, or more to taste

For the Sauce:
2 tablespoons prepared horseradish
1/4 cup sour cream
2 tablespoons mayonnaise

Directions

- Toss the chuck with bay leaves, vegetable oil, garlic, Italian seasoning, mustard, red wine, salt, black pepper and cayenne pepper.
- Let it marinate overnight in the refrigerator. Place your chuck in a baking dish that is lined with a piece of foil; pour the marinade over it.
- Wrap with the foil. Then, bake at 375 degrees F for 2 hours or until a thermometer registers 125 degrees F.
- In the meantime, mix all ingredients for the sauce. Slice your chuck across the grain. Let cool completely.

Storing

Divide the meat between three airtight containers or Ziploc bags; keep in your refrigerator for 3 to 4 days. Place the horseradish sauce in an airtight container and keep in your refrigerator for up to 4 days.
For freezing, place the meat in airtight containers or heavy-duty freezer bags. Freeze up to 2 to 3 months. Defrost in the refrigerator. Enjoy!

69. Crock Pot Beef Brisket with Blue Cheese

Ready in about 8 hours
Servings 6

Beef brisket is an amazing dish because it turns great every time! Additionally, you can use leftovers, cold or warm, for sandwiches, dips, and salads.

Per serving: 397 Calories; 31.4g Fat; 3.9g Carbs; 23.5g Protein; 2.3g Sugars

Ingredients

2 tablespoons olive oil
1 shallot, chopped
1/2 tablespoon garlic paste
1 ½ pounds corned beef brisket
1/4 teaspoon cloves, ground
1/3 teaspoon ground coriander
1/4 cup soy sauce
1 cup water
6 ounces blue cheese, crumbled

Directions

- Heat a sauté pan with the olive oil over medium heat. Cook the shallot until it is softened.
- Add garlic paste and cook an additional minute; transfer to your Crock pot that is previously greased with a nonstick cooking spray.
- Sear the brisket until it has a golden-brown crust. Transfer to the Crock pot. Add the remaining ingredient, except for blue cheese.
- Cover and cook on Low heat setting for 6 to 8 hours or until the meat is very tender. Garnish with blue cheese. Let cool completely.

Storing

Divide the meat between three airtight containers or Ziploc bags; keep in your refrigerator for 3 to 5 days. For freezing, place the meat in airtight containers or heavy-duty freezer bags. Freeze up to 3 months. Defrost in the refrigerator. Enjoy!

70. Filet Mignon Steaks with Wine Sauce

Ready in about 30 minutes
Servings 4

Need more ideas for what to make with beef steaks? Try these filet mignon steaks for an easy mid-week meal.

Per serving: 451 Calories; 34.4g Fat; 3.6g Carbs; 29.7g Protein; 1.2g Sugars

Ingredients

4 (6-ounce) filet mignon steaks
1 tablespoon deli mustard
Celery salt and freshly ground pepper, to taste
2 rosemary sprigs
1 thyme sprigs
2 tablespoons lard, room temperature
1 cup scallions, chopped
2 garlic cloves, minced
1 red bell pepper, deveined and chopped
1/2 cup dry red wine

Directions

- Rub filet mignon steaks with mustard. Sprinkle filet mignon steaks with the salt, pepper, rosemary and thyme.
- Heat the lard in a heavy-bottomed skillet over a moderate heat. Cook filet mignon steaks for 10 minutes on each side or until a thermometer registers 120 degrees F.
- Now, cook the scallions, garlic, and pepper in pan drippings about 3 minutes. Pour in the wine to scrape up any browned bits from the bottom of the skillet.
- Now, cook until the liquid is reduced by half. Let cool completely.

Storing

Divide the steaks along with the sauce between four airtight containers or Ziploc bags; keep in your refrigerator for up to 3 to 4 days.
For freezing, place the steaks in airtight containers or heavy-duty freezer bags. Freeze up to 3 months. Defrost in the refrigerator. Bon appétit!

71. Spicy Winter Sauerkraut with Ground Beef

Ready in about 20 minutes
Servings 4

Sauerkraut is loaded with dietary fiber, vitamin C, vitamin A, and vitamin K. In addition, it contains a significant amount of magnesium, iron, manganese, copper, and calcium.

Per serving: 330 Calories; 12.2g Fat; 8.7g Carbs; 44.4g Protein; 3.6g Sugars

Ingredients

1 tablespoon tallow, melted
2 onions, chopped
2 garlic cloves, smashed
1 ¼ pounds ground beef
18 ounces sauerkraut, rinsed and well drained
1 teaspoon chili pepper flakes
1 teaspoon mustard powder
1 bay leaf
Sea salt and ground black pepper, to taste

Directions

- Heat a saucepan over a moderately high heat. Now, warm the tallow and cook the onions and garlic until aromatic.
- Stir in ground beef and cook until it is slightly browned.
- Add the remaining ingredients. Reduce the heat to medium. Cook about 6 minutes or until everything is thoroughly cooked. Let cool completely.

Storing

Divide the sauerkraut between four airtight containers or Ziploc bags; keep in your refrigerator for up to 3 to 5 days.
For freezing, place the steaks in airtight containers or heavy-duty freezer bags. Freeze up to 5 months. Defrost in the refrigerator. Bon appétit!

72. Hamburger Soup with Cabbage

Ready in about 35 minutes
Servings 4

If you feel like simplifying things, this recipe will be your next favorite. This soup freezes and reheats well so you can make a double batch.

Per serving: 307 Calories; 23.6g Fat; 8.4g Carbs; 14.8g Protein; 3.2g Sugars

Ingredients

2 tablespoons lard, melted
3/4 pound ground chuck
1/2 cup scallions, chopped
2 cloves garlic, minced
1 carrot, diced
1 cup cabbage, shredded
1 celery with leaves, diced
1 tomato, pureed
6 cups chicken broth
1 bay leaf
Seasoned salt and ground black pepper, to taste
1 cup sour cream

Directions

- Melt the lard in a stockpot. Cook the chuck until it is no longer pink; reserve.
- Then, cook the scallions, garlic, carrot, cabbage, and celery in the pan drippings, stirring constantly.
- Stir in the other ingredients along with reserved chuck, bringing to a rapid boil. Turn the heat to a simmer. Cook another 27 minutes, partially covered.
- Taste and adjust the seasonings. Ladle into individual bowls; garnish with full-fat sour cream. Let cool completely.

Storing

Spoon the soup into four airtight containers or Ziploc bags; keep in your refrigerator for up to 3 to 4 days.
For freezing, place the soup in airtight containers. It will maintain the best quality for about 4 to 6 months. Defrost in the refrigerator. Bon appétit!

73. Hearty Pollock Chowder

Ready in about 30 minutes
Servings 4

The best of vegetable and fish chowders come together in one super-healthy dish! It would be great if you could find hickory smoke salt for this recipe.

Per serving: 170 Calories; 5.8g Fat; 8.7g Carbs; 20g Protein; 4.2g Sugars

Ingredients

1 ¼ pounds pollock fillets, skin removed
3 teaspoons butter
2 shallots, chopped
1 celery with leaves, chopped
1 parsnip, chopped
2 carrots, chopped
Sea salt and ground black pepper, to taste
1 teaspoon Old Bay seasonings
3 cups boiling water
1/2 cup clam juice
1/4 cup dry white wine
1/2 cup full-fat milk

Directions

- Chop pollock fillets into bite-sized pieces.
- Warm the butter in a pan over a moderately high flame. Cook the vegetables until they're softened. Season with salt, pepper and Old Bay seasonings.
- Stir in chopped fish and cook for 12 to 15 minutes more. Add the boiling water and clam juice. Afterwards, pour in the white wine and milk.
- Bring to a boil. Reduce the heat and cook for 15 minutes longer. Let cool completely.

Storing

Spoon the chowder into four airtight containers or Ziploc bags; keep in your refrigerator for up to 3 to 4 days.
For freezing, place the chowder in airtight containers. It will maintain the best quality for about 4 months. Defrost in the refrigerator. Bon appétit!

74. Winter Chanterelle and Leek Stew

Ready in about 25 minutes
Servings 4

Chanterelle, also known as "egg mushroom", is a fleshy wild mushroom with many health benefits. They are loaded with vitamin B, protein, selenium, zinc, and potassium. Enjoy!

Per serving: 114 Calories; 7.3g Fat; 10g Carbs; 2.1g Protein; 4.3g Sugars

Ingredients

2 tablespoons olive oil
1 cup leeks, chopped
2 garlic cloves, pressed
1/2 cup celery with leaves, chopped
2 carrots, chopped
1 cup fresh Chanterelle, sliced
2 tablespoons dry red wine
2 rosemary sprigs, chopped
1 thyme sprig, chopped
3 ½ cups roasted vegetable stock
1/2 teaspoon cayenne pepper
1 teaspoon Hungarian paprika
2 ripe tomatoes, pureed
1 tablespoon flaxseed meal

Directions

- Heat the oil in a stockpot over a moderate flame. Now, cook the leeks until they are tender.
- Add garlic, celery, and carrots and cook for a further 4 minutes or until they are softened.
- Now, stir in Chanterelle mushrooms; cook until they lose their liquid; reserve the vegetables.
- Pour in the wine to deglaze the bottom of the stockpot. Now, add rosemary and thyme.
- Add roasted vegetable stock, cayenne pepper, Hungarian paprika, and tomatoes; stir in reserved vegetables and bring to a boil.
- Reduce heat to a simmer. Let it simmer, covered, an additional 15 minutes. Add flaxseed meal to thicken the soup. Let cool completely.

Storing

Spoon the stew into four airtight containers or Ziploc bags; keep in your refrigerator for up to 3 to 4 days.
For freezing, place the stew in airtight containers. Freeze up to 4 to 6 months. Defrost in the refrigerator. Bon appétit!

75. One-Pot Seafood Stew

Ready in about 20 minutes
Servings 4

This seafood stew might become one of your favorite family recipes of all time! This amazing stew reheats well.

Per serving: 209 Calories; 12.6g Fat; 7.6g Carbs; 15.2g Protein; 3.1g Sugars

Ingredients

1/2 stick butter, at room temperature
2 onions, chopped
2 garlic cloves, pressed
2 tomatoes, pureed
1 celery stalk, chopped
2 cups shellfish stock
1 cup hot water
2 tablespoons dry white wine
1/2 teaspoon lemon zest
1/2 pound shrimp
1/2 pound mussels
1 teaspoon Italian seasonings
1 teaspoon saffron threads
Salt and ground black pepper, to taste

Directions

- Melt the butter in a stockpot over a moderate heat. Cook the onion and garlic until aromatic.
- Now, stir in pureed tomatoes; cook for 8 minutes or until heated through.
- Add the remaining ingredients and bring to a rapid boil. Reduce the heat to a simmer and cook an additional 4 minutes.
- Let cool completely.

Storing

Spoon the stew into four airtight containers or Ziploc bags; keep in your refrigerator for up to 3 to 4 days. For freezing, place the stew in airtight containers. Freeze up to 4 to 6 months. Defrost in the refrigerator. Bon appétit!

76. Creole Salmon Fillets

Ready in about 40 minutes
Servings 4

Looking for a last-minute recipe for a family gathering? Richly flavored with seasonings and marinated in a blend of Worcestershire sauce, lime juice and avocado oil, this gourmet dish will amaze your family!

Per serving: 266 Calories; 11.5g Fat; 5.6g Carbs; 34.9g Protein; 4.2g Sugars

Ingredients

1/3 cup fresh lime juice
1/3 cup Worcestershire sauce
3 teaspoons avocado oil
1/4 cup fresh chives, chopped
2 garlic cloves, minced
1/4 teaspoon onion powder
1 teaspoon lemon thyme
1/4 teaspoon ground black pepper
1/4 teaspoon white pepper
1 teaspoon dried oregano
4 salmon fillets

Directions

- To make the marinade, thoroughly mix the lime juice, Worcestershire sauce, avocado oil, fresh chives, garlic, and onion powder.
- Place the salmon fillets in the marinade; place in the refrigerator for 20 to 25 minutes. Season the salmon fillets with lemon thyme, black pepper, white pepper and oregano.
- Place the salmon fillets on the preheated grill and reserve the marinade.
- Cook your salmon for 10 to 12 minutes, turning once and brushing with the reserved marinade.
- Let cool completely.

Storing

Divide salmon fillets between four airtight containers; keep in your refrigerator for up to 3 to 4 days.
For freezing, place them in airtight containers or wrap tightly with freezer wrap. Freeze up to 2 to 3 months. Defrost in the refrigerator. Bon appétit!

77. Pork Ribs with Roasted Peppers

Ready in about 2 hours
Servings 4

The perfect mix of flavors and textures in this oven-roasted pork dish will amaze your family and friends. Don't be shy about seasonings and enjoy experimenting with them.

Per serving: 370 Calories; 21.3g Fat; 8.3g Carbs; 33.7g Protein; 3.7g Sugars

Ingredients

2 tablespoons olive oil
1 pound baby back ribs
Salt and pepper, to your liking
1 tablespoon garlic paste
1 red onion, chopped
2 rosemary sprigs
1 tablespoon crushed sage
1 tablespoon tamarind paste
1 cup beef broth
1/2 cup dry sherry
1/2 cup soy sauce
2 roasted red bell peppers, chopped
2 roasted chile peppers, chopped

Directions

- Start by preheating your oven to 340 degrees F. Spritz a roasting pan with a nonstick cooking spray.
- Heat the oil in an ovenproof pan over a moderately high heat. Now, brown the meat on all sides for 10 minutes; sprinkle with salt and pepper.
- Add the garlic paste, onion, rosemary and sage. Cook an additional 4 minutes or until heated through. Stir in the remaining ingredients.
- Bake for 1 hour 30 minutes in the middle of the preheated oven. Let cool completely.

Storing

Divide baby back ribs into four portions. Place each portion of ribs along with roasted peppers in an airtight container; keep in your refrigerator for 3 to 5 days.
For freezing, place the ribs in airtight containers or heavy-duty freezer bags. Freeze up to 4 to 6 months. Defrost in the refrigerator. Reheat in your oven at 250 degrees F until heated through. Bon appétit!

78. Pan-Seared Pork Steaks

Ready in about 30 minutes
Servings 4

Pork steak, also known as Boston butt or pork blade steak, is a pork cut that is high in protein and low in carbs. Serve as an easy family lunch or a protein-packed dinner.

Per serving: 305 Calories; 20.6g Fat; 3.7g Carbs; 22.5g Protein; 1.3g Sugars

Ingredients

2 tablespoons lard, room temperature
4 pork butt steaks
1/4 cup dry red wine
1 teaspoon celery seeds
1/2 teaspoon cayenne pepper
1/2 teaspoon salt
1/2 teaspoon freshly ground black pepper
1 red onion, peeled and chopped
1 garlic clove, minced

Directions

- Melt 1 tablespoon of lard in a cast-iron skillet that is preheated over a moderate heat. Cover the skillet and sear the butt steaks for 10 minutes on each side.
- Add a splash of red wine to deglaze the pot. Season with celery seeds, cayenne pepper, salt and black pepper; cook an additional 8 to 12 minutes; reserve.
- Warm remaining 1 tablespoon of lard in the same skillet; cook the onions and garlic until tender and aromatic. Let cool completely.

Storing

Divide the steaks and vegetables between four airtight containers or Ziploc bags; keep in your refrigerator for up to 3 to 5 days.
For freezing, place the steaks in airtight containers or heavy-duty freezer bags. Freeze up to 4 months. Defrost in the refrigerator. Bon appétit!

79. Spicy Pork Soup

Ready in about 1 hour
Servings 4

Anaheim chile adds a distinctive twist to this recipe. It is a mild hot pepper that can be replaced with poblano peppers or serrano pepper, which are tangier than Anaheim, with more earthy flavor.

Per serving: 341 Calories; 12.9g Fat; 8.8g Carbs; 45.4g Protein; 3.3g Sugars

Ingredients

2 tablespoons olive oil
1 ½ pounds pork stew meat, cubed
Salt and black pepper, to taste
1 onion, chopped
2 garlic cloves, crushed
1/2 cup dry white wine
2 carrots, thinly sliced
2 parsnips, thinly sliced
4 cups beef bone broth
1 ripe Roma tomato, crushed
1 Anaheim chile, seeded and cut into very thin strips with scissors
1/2 teaspoon dried basil
2 thyme sprigs
2 rosemary sprigs
Fresh cilantro, for garnish

Directions

- Heat olive oil in a heavy-bottomed pot that is preheated over a moderately high flame. Now, sear the pork cubes until they are just browned; reserve.
- Then, cook the onions and garlic in pan drippings for 3 to 4 minutes. Pour in wine to deglaze the bottom.
- Add the carrots, parsnip, and beef bone broth, bringing to a boil. Turn the heat to medium-low and simmer 6 to 7 more minutes.
- Add tomato, chile, basil, thyme, and rosemary; let it simmer an additional 50 minutes, partially covered. Garnish with chopped cilantro. Let cool completely.

Storing

Spoon the soup into four airtight containers or Ziploc bags; keep in your refrigerator for up to 3 to 4 days. For freezing, place the soup in airtight containers. Freeze up to 4 to 6 months. Defrost in the refrigerator. Bon appétit!

80. Mom's Signature Pork Stew

Ready in about 25 minutes
Servings 4

Here is a foolproof pork recipe that is sure to please any crowd! It is worth the invested time, trust me.

Per serving: 295 Calories; 19.6g Fat; 10.7g Carbs; 20.3g Protein; 2.6g Sugars

Ingredients

1 tablespoon butter
2 shallots, chopped
1 carrot, chopped
1 teaspoon habanero pepper, deveined and minced
3/4 pound boneless pork shoulder, cubed
1/2 tablespoon garlic paste
1 ½ cups bone broth
1/2 teaspoon ground bay leaf
1/2 teaspoon ground cloves
Himalayan salt and ground black pepper, to taste
1 tablespoon fresh parsley, chopped
1 avocado, pitted, peeled and diced
1/2 cup sour cream, full-fat

Directions

- Melt the butter in a heavy-bottomed pot that is preheated over a moderate heat.
- Now, sauté the shallots, carrot, and habanero pepper for 3 minutes or until they are tender.
- After that, add cubed pork; cook an additional 5 minutes, stirring frequently.
- Then, add the garlic paste, broth, bay leaf powder ground cloves, salt, and pepper; turn the heat to a medium-high and bring it to a boil.
- Next, decrease the heat to a simmer. Cook an additional 15 minutes or until thoroughly heated.
- Garnish with fresh parsley, avocado and sour cream. Let cool completely.

Storing

Spoon the stew into four airtight containers or Ziploc bags; keep in your refrigerator for up to 3 to 4 days. For freezing, place the stew in airtight containers. Freeze up to 4 to 6 months. Defrost in the refrigerator. Bon appétit!

DINNER

81. Chinese-Style Turkey Meatballs

Ready in about 20 minutes
Servings 4

These tender and mouthwatering meatballs can be served on any occasion. Don't forget to add a pinch of Sichuan peppercorn for some extra oomph!

Per serving: 244 Calories; 13.7g Fat; 5g Carbs; 27.6g Protein; 3.2g Sugars

Ingredients

For the Meatballs:
3/4 pound ground turkey
1 egg
1/3 cup cheddar cheese, freshly grated
1/3 teaspoon black pepper
1/3 teaspoon Five-spice powder

For the Sauce:
1 1/3 cups water
1/3 cup red wine vinegar
2 tablespoons Worcestershire sauce
1/2 cup tomato puree, sugar-free
1/2 teaspoon cayenne pepper
3/4 cup erythritol
1/3 teaspoon guar gum

Directions

- Thoroughly combine ground turkey, the egg, cheese, black pepper and Five-spice powder in a mixing bowl. Now, form the mixture into balls (about 28 meatballs).
- Preheat a nonstick skillet over a medium heat. Brown your meatballs on all sides for 3 to 4 minutes; set them aside.
- Next, add the water, vinegar, Worcestershire sauce, tomato puree, cayenne pepper and erythritol to the skillet. Whisk until well mixed.
- After that, gradually add the guar gum. Whisk until the sauce is thickened. Decrease the temperature and bring the sauce to a simmer; make sure to stir periodically.
- Add the meatballs to the sauce; continue to simmer for 8 to 12 minutes on low or until your meatballs are thoroughly cooked. Let cool completely.

Storing

Place meatballs along with the sauce in airtight containers or Ziploc bags; keep in your refrigerator for up to 3 to 4 days.
Freeze the meatballs in the sauce in airtight containers or heavy-duty freezer bags. Freeze up to 3 to 4 months. To defrost, slowly reheat in a saucepan. Bon appétit!

82. Parmesan Breaded Chicken Breasts with Peppers

Ready in about 30 minutes
Servings 4

A keto-style chicken tastes so good! Especially when served with roasted bell peppers. Just replace regular breadcrumbs with crushed pork rinds. Clever!

Per serving: 367 Calories; 16.9g Fat; 9g Carbs; 43g Protein; 6g Sugars

Ingredients

1 pound chicken breasts, butterflied
1 teaspoon salt
1/4 teaspoon ground black pepper, or more to taste
1 teaspoon fresh or dried dill, chopped
1/3 cup crushed pork rinds
1/3 cup Parmigiano-Reggiano, freshly grated
2 teaspoons vegetable oil
1 garlic clove, minced
3 bell peppers, quartered lengthwise

Directions

- Begin by preheating your oven to 420 degrees F. Cover the sides and bottom of a baking pan with a sheet of foil.
- Place butterflied chicken breast on the baking pan. Season with salt and pepper.
- Now, combine dill, pork rinds, Parmigiano-Reggiano, vegetable oil and garlic clove. Dip each chicken breast into this mixture.
- Arrange bell peppers around the prepared chicken breasts. Bake for 20 minutes or until juices run clear. Let cool completely.

Storing

Place breaded chicken breasts along with peppers in airtight containers or Ziploc bags; keep in your refrigerator for up 1 to 2 days.
For freezing, place them in airtight containers or heavy-duty freezer bags. Freeze up to 2 to 3 months. Defrost in the refrigerator or microwave. Enjoy!

83. Prosciutto-Wrapped Chicken with Cottage Cheese

Ready in about 35 minutes
Servings 2

You don't need to be an expert chef to make this tasty, gourmet chicken dish. Your family will be delighted!

Per serving: 499 Calories; 18.9g Fat; 5.7g Carbs; 41.6g Protein; 3.2g Sugars

Ingredients

1 chicken breasts, boneless, skinless and flattened
1 teaspoon smoked paprika
Salt and ground black pepper, to taste pepper
1/2 cup Cottage cheese
1 tablespoon fresh cilantro, chopped
4 slices of prosciutto

Directions

- Start by preheating your oven to 390 degrees F. Line a baking pan with parchment paper.
- Season chicken breasts with smoked paprika, salt and pepper. Spread Cottage cheese over chicken breasts; scatter fresh cilantro over the top.
- Roll up and cut into 4 pieces. Now, wrap each piece with one slice of prosciutto; secure with a toothpick.
- Place the wrapped chicken in the baking pan; bake for 25 to 35 minutes. Let cool completely.

Storing

Place chicken in airtight containers or Ziploc bags; keep in your refrigerator for 3 to 4 days.
For freezing, place them in airtight containers or heavy-duty freezer bags. Freeze up to 4 months. Defrost in the refrigerator. Enjoy!

84. Roasted Chicken Wings with Cashew-Basil Pesto

Ready in about 35 minutes
Servings 4

Hot or cold, these chicken wings taste delicious! When it comes to the pesto, use roasted salted cashews for the best results.

Per serving: 580 Calories; 44.8g Fat; 8g Carbs; 38.7g Protein; 1.5g Sugars

Ingredients

1 pound chicken wings, skinless
Salt and ground black pepper, to taste
1 teaspoon cayenne pepper
1 cup scallions

For the Cashew-Basil Pesto:
1/2 cup fresh basil leaves
2 garlic cloves, minced
1/2 cup cashews
1/2 cup Romano cheese
1/2 cup olive oil

Directions

- Begin by preheating your oven to 392 degrees F. Rub the chicken wings with the salt, black pepper, and cayenne pepper.
- Arrange chicken wings in a lightly greased baking dish; scatter scallions around the chicken.
- Roast for 30 minutes, turning the baking dish once.
- In a food processor, pulse basil, garlic, cashews and Romano cheese. Add the oil in a constant tiny stream. Season with sea salt to taste. Garnish with roasted scallions. Let cool completely.

Storing

Place chicken wings in airtight containers or Ziploc bags; keep in your refrigerator for up 3 to 4 days.
Place pesto sauce in an airtight glass jar. Store in the refrigerator for up to a week.
To freeze chicken wings, place them in airtight containers or heavy-duty freezer bags. Freeze up to 3 months. Once thawed in the refrigerator, heat in the preheated oven at 375 degrees F for 20 to 25 minutes.
Freeze pesto in lightly oiled ice cube trays; once frozen, place in an airtight container in your freezer. Bon appétit!

85. Mediterranean Chicken Breasts

Ready in about 40 minutes
Servings 8

These chicken breasts are healthy and they taste so divine! Best of all, you only need 40 minutes to get your keto dinner ready!

Per serving: 306 Calories; 17.8g Fat; 3.1g Carbs; 31.7g Protein; 1.3g Sugars

Ingredients

4 chicken breasts, skinless and boneless
2 garlic cloves, pressed
1 teaspoon dried oregano
1/2 teaspoon dried basil
2 sprigs thyme
1 sprig rosemary
Salt and ground black pepper, to taste
2 tablespoons peanut oil
1 bell pepper, deveined and thinly sliced
10 Kalamata olives, pitted
1 ½ cups chicken stock

Directions

- Rub chicken breast with the garlic and seasonings. Heat the peanut oil in a pan that is preheated over a moderately high heat.
- Now, fry the chicken until it is browned on all sides, for 4 to 6 minutes.
- Add the remaining ingredients; bring it to boil. Reduce the heat to medium-low. Continue cooking, partially covered, for 30 minutes. Let cool completely.

Storing

Place chicken breasts in airtight containers or Ziploc bags; keep in your refrigerator for 3 to 4 days.
For freezing, place them in airtight containers or heavy-duty freezer bags. It will maintain the best quality for about 4 months. Defrost in the refrigerator.
Enjoy!

86. Pork Belly with Homey Barbecue Sauce

Ready in about 2 hours
Servings 8

Pork belly is the queen of low-carb foods. Serve with a selection of seasonal vegetables.

Per serving: 561 Calories; 34g Fat; 1.7g Carbs; 52.7g Protein; 0.8g Sugars

Ingredients

2 pounds pork belly
2 tablespoons vegetable oil
2 garlic cloves, halved
1 teaspoon salt
1/2 teaspoon freshly ground black pepper
For the Barbecue Sauce:
1/2 cup tomato puree
1 teaspoon hot sauce
1 teaspoon Dijon mustard
A few drops of liquid smoke
1/3 teaspoon ground cumin
1/3 teaspoon smoked paprika

Directions

- Preheat your oven to 420 degrees F.
- Now, rub the pork belly with vegetable oil and garlic. Sprinkle with salt and pepper.
- Roast the pork for 18 to 22 minutes. Now, decrease the heat to 330 degrees F. Roast for a further 1 hour 30 minutes.
- Meanwhile, whisk all ingredients for the barbecue sauce until everything is well blended. Remove the crackling and cut the pork belly into slices. Let cool completely.

Storing

Place the pork pieces into four airtight containers or Ziploc bags; keep in your refrigerator for 3 to 4 days.
For freezing, wrap tightly with heavy-duty aluminum foil or freezer wrap. It will maintain the best quality for 2 to 3 months. Defrost in the refrigerator.
Place the sauce in an airtight container and keep it in your refrigerator for a week. You can also freeze it for about a month. Enjoy!

87. Juicy Pork Medallions with Scallions

Ready in about 20 minutes
Servings 4

Pan-seared pork medallions are perfect when served over fresh salad or a cauliflower rice. Add Mediterranean herbs and experience an unbelievable burst of flavor.

Per serving: 192 Calories; 6.9g Fat; 0.9g Carbs; 29.8g Protein; 0.4g Sugars

Ingredients

1 pound pork tenderloin, cut crosswise into 12 medallions
Coarse salt and ground black pepper, to taste
1/2 teaspoon garlic powder
1/2 teaspoon red pepper flakes, crushed
1 tablespoon butter
A bunch of scallions, roughly chopped
1 thyme sprig, minced
2 rosemary sprigs, minced
1 teaspoon dried sage, crushed

Directions

- Season each pork medallion with salt, black pepper, garlic powder and red pepper flakes.
- Then, melt the butter in a saucepan over medium-high heat. Cook pork tenderloin about 3 minutes per side.
- Add the scallions, thyme, and rosemary; cook until heated through, an additional 3 minutes. Garnish with dried sage. Let cool completely.

Storing

Divide pork medallions and veggies into four portions; place each portion in a separate airtight container or Ziploc bag; keep in your refrigerator for 3 to 4 days.
Freeze the pork medallions and veggies in airtight containers or heavy-duty freezer bags. Freeze up to 4 months.
Remove the pork medallions and veggies from the freezer and place them in the refrigerator. Reheat the pork cutlets in the same way you prepared them, if possible. Bon appétit!

88. Crock Pot Peppery Pork Ribs

Ready in about 8 hours
Servings 4

The grandma's secret to the perfect pork chops – go nicely and slowly. Don't forget to add the driest red wine you can find like Merlo, Cabernet Sauvignon, Shiraz or Pinot Noir. Enjoy!

Per serving: 192 Calories; 6.9g Fat; 0.9g Carbs; 29.8g Protein; 0.4g Sugars

Ingredients

1 tablespoon lard
1 pound pork ribs
1 teaspoon Ancho chiles, minced
1 bell pepper, thinly sliced
1/4 cup Worcestershire sauce
1/4 cup dry red wine
1/2 teaspoon smoked cayenne pepper
1 garlic clove, crushed
1/2 teaspoon ground oregano
1/2 teaspoon ground cloves
1 teaspoon grated orange peel

Directions

- Treat the sides and bottom of your Crock pot with melted lard. Arrange pork chops and peppers on the bottom.
- Drizzle Worcestershire sauce and wine over everything. Sprinkle with cayenne pepper, garlic, oregano and ground cloves.
- Slow cook on Low setting approximately 8 hours. Garnish with grated orange peel. Let cool completely.

Storing

Divide ribs into four portions. Place each portion of ribs along with roasted peppers in an airtight container; keep in your refrigerator for 3 to 5 days.
For freezing, place the ribs in airtight containers or heavy-duty freezer bags. Freeze up to 4 to 6 months.
Defrost in the refrigerator. Reheat in your oven at 250 degrees F until heated through. Bon appétit!

89. Pork Chops with Ancho Chile Sauce

Ready in about 30 minutes
Servings 6

Is there anything better than juicy pork chops with a hot, spicy sauce? This pork dish might earn a permanent spot in your keto meal plan.

Per serving: 347 Calories; 29.2g Fat; 0.2g Carbs; 20.2g Protein; 0.2g Sugars

Ingredients

1 tablespoon olive oil
6 pork chops

For the Sauce:
2 Ancho chiles, chopped
1/2 cup bone broth
2 garlic cloves, minced
1/2 teaspoon ground cumin
1 teaspoon dried basil
1/2 teaspoon red pepper flakes, crushed
Salt and ground black pepper, to taste
2 teaspoons olive oil

Directions

- Heat 1 tablespoon of olive oil in a saucepan that is preheated over a moderately high flame. Sear the pork chops until they're well browned and their juices run clear.
- To make the sauce, in a pot, boil Ancho chiles and bone broth for a couple of minutes. Now, remove your pot from the heat; allow the chiles to stand in the hot water for 15 to 25 minutes.
- Add the chiles along with the liquid to a blender or food processor; add the remaining ingredients for the sauce.
- Puree until creamy, smooth and uniform. Let cool completely.

Storing

Divide pork chops and sauce into six portions; place each portion in a separate airtight container or Ziploc bag; keep in your refrigerator for 3 to 4 days.
Freeze the pork chops in sauce in airtight containers or heavy-duty freezer bags. Freeze up to 4 months. Defrost in the refrigerator. Bon appétit!

90. Spicy Habanero and Ground Beef Dinner

Ready in about 40 minutes
Servings 6

This beef dish is easy to make and easy to eat! How could it be any better than this?!

Per serving: 361 Calories; 21.9g Fat; 8.4g Carbs; 29g Protein; 1.5g Sugars

Ingredients

2 tablespoons tallow, at room temperature
1 ½ pounds ground chuck
1/4 teaspoon caraway seeds, ground
1/2 teaspoon dried basil
1/2 teaspoon dried thyme
1/2 teaspoon paprika
1/2 teaspoon ground bay leaf
1 teaspoon fennel seeds
1/2 teaspoon salt
1/2 teaspoon ground black pepper
2 shallots, chopped
2 garlic cloves, minced
1 teaspoon habanero pepper, minced
2 ripe Roma tomatoes, crushed
1/2 cup dry sherry wine

For Ketogenic Tortillas:
4 egg whites
1/4 cup coconut flour
1/3 teaspoon baking powder
6 tablespoons water
A pinch of table salt
A pinch of Swerve

Directions

- Melt the tallow in a wok that is preheated over a moderately high heat.
- Now, brown the ground chuck for 4 minutes, crumbling it with a fork. Add all seasonings along with shallots, garlic, and habanero pepper. Continue to cook 9 minutes longer.
- Now, stir in the tomatoes and sherry. Now, turn the heat to medium-low, cover, and let it simmer an additional 20 minutes.
- Meanwhile, make the tortillas by mixing the eggs, coconut flour and baking powder in a bowl. Add the water, salt and Swerve and mix until everything is well incorporated.
- Preheat a nonstick skillet over a moderate flame. Bake tortillas for a couple of minutes on each side. Repeat until you run out of batter. Let cool completely.

Storing

Place the ground meat mixture in airtight containers; keep in your refrigerator for 3 to 4 days.
Freeze the ground meat mixture in airtight containers or heavy-duty freezer bags. Freeze up to 2 to 3 months.
Defrost them in the refrigerator and reheat in the microwave.
Cover tortillas with foil to prevent drying out; keep in the refrigerator for 1 to 2 days. For freezing, place a sheet of wax paper between each tortilla; then, wrap tortillas tightly in foil; freeze up to 2 months. Bon appétit!

91. Beef Sausage with Mayo Sauce

Ready in about 15 minutes
Servings 4

Enjoy this "good-for-you" meal that is chock-full of gourmet sausage, great aromatics, and amazing sauce. This is the perfect idea for those short on time.

Per serving: 549 Calories; 49.3g Fat; 9.7g Carbs; 16.2g Protein; 2.3g Sugars

Ingredients

1 tablespoon lard, at room temperature
1 red onion, chopped
1 garlic clove, finely minced
1 pound beef sausage, crumbled
1/2 teaspoon salt
1/3 teaspoon red pepper flakes
1/2 teaspoon dried marjoram
2 tablespoons cilantro, minced

For the Sauce:
1/4 cup mayonnaise
1 tablespoon tomato puree
1 ½ teaspoon mustard
1 teaspoon cayenne pepper
A pinch of salt

Directions

- Melt the lard over medium-high heat. Add the onion and garlic and cook for 2 minutes or until tender and fragrant.
- Stir in the beef and continue to cook for about 3 minutes more. Stir in the salt, red pepper, marjoram and cilantro; cook for 1 more minute.
- Then, make the sauce by whisking all the sauce ingredients. Let cool completely.

Storing

Divide sausage into four portions. Place each portion in an airtight container; keep in your refrigerator for 3 to 4 days.
For freezing, wrap sausages tightly with heavy-duty aluminum foil or freezer wrap. Freeze up to 1 to 2 months. Defrost in the refrigerator.
Place the sauce in an airtight glass jar; keep in your refrigerator for 2 to 3 days. Enjoy!

92. Slow Cooker Beef Chuck Roast

Ready in about 6 hours
Servings 8

This super tender beef chuck roast will win your table! Serve with a horseradish sauce.

Per serving: 519 Calories; 39.6g Fat; 2.7g Carbs; 34.4g Protein; 1.4g Sugars

Ingredients

2 pounds beef chuck roast
2 tablespoons olive oil
1 large-sized white onion, cut into wedges
3 garlic cloves, minced
2 rosemary springs
1 thyme sprig
1/3 cup dry red wine
Salt and pepper to taste
2 tablespoons Worcestershire sauce
1/2 cup beef broth
2 tablespoons fresh parsley, chopped
1 cup Provolone, sliced

Directions

- Add the beef, olive oil, onion, garlic, rosemary and thyme to your Crock pot.
- Now, add dry red wine, salt, pepper, Worcestershire sauce, beef broth.
- Cover and cook on High settings until meat is tender, about 6 hours.
- Garnish with fresh parsley and sliced Provolone cheese. Let cool completely.

Storing

Divide the beef chuck roast into eight portions; place each portion in an airtight container or Ziploc bag; keep in your refrigerator for 3 to 4 days.
For freezing, place the meat in airtight containers or heavy-duty freezer bags. Freeze up to 2 to 3 months. Defrost in the refrigerator. Bon appétit!

93. Oven Roasted Rib-Eye Steak

Ready in about 25 minutes
Servings 6

Keep in mind that thinner steak actually shortens the cooking time. Therefore, try to purchase the steak that is about one-inch thick.

Per serving: 343 Calories; 27.3g Fat; 3g Carbs; 20.1g Protein; 0g Sugars

Ingredients

1 tablespoon vegetable oil
1 ½ pounds rib-eye steak
1 teaspoon sea salt
1/2 teaspoon ground black pepper
2 garlic cloves, minced
1/2 cup Worcester sauce
2 tablespoons apple cider vinegar

Directions

- Preheat your oven to 350 degrees F. Grease a roasting pan with a nonstick cooking spray.
- Heat vegetable oil in a skillet that is preheated over a medium-high heat. Season the steak with salt and black pepper; sear the steak until just browned or about 3 minutes.
- Place the steak in the prepared roasting pan. In a mixing bowl, combine the garlic, Worcester sauce and apple cider vinegar. Pour this mixture over the steak.
- Afterwards, cover tightly with a piece of foil. Roast the steak about 20 minutes or until it is tender and well browned. Let cool completely.

Storing

Cut the steak into six pieces; divide the pieces between six airtight containers; keep in your refrigerator for up to 3 to 4 days.
For freezing, place the steaks in airtight containers or heavy-duty freezer bags. Freeze up to 2 to 3 months. Defrost in the refrigerator. Bon appétit!

94. Broccoli and Ground Beef Delight

Ready in about 20 minutes
Servings 4

Treat your family and guests to a plate chock-full of lovely meat, vegetable and aromatics. Serve with a homemade low-carb bread.

Per serving: 241 Calories; 7.6g Fat; 6g Carbs; 36g Protein; 1.9g Sugars

Ingredients

2 teaspoons avocado oil
1 head broccoli, cut into small florets
1 teaspoon garlic, minced
1 cup red onion, sliced
1 pound ground beef
1/2 teaspoon salt
1/2 ground black pepper
1/4 teaspoon cayenne pepper
1/2 cup beef bone broth
2 tablespoons Marsala wine
1/2 teaspoon dill weed
1/2 teaspoon turmeric

Directions

- Heat 1 teaspoon of avocado oil in a pan that is preheated over a moderate flame. Then, cook the broccoli for 3 to 4 minutes, stirring often.
- Now, stir in the garlic and onion; cook until aromatic and just tender, or about 2 minutes. Reserve.
- Heat another teaspoon of avocado oil. Stir in the beef and cook until it is well browned.
- Add the reserved broccoli mixture, lower the heat and add the remaining ingredients. Cook, covered, until everything is heated through, or about 10 minutes. Let cool completely.

Storing

Divide the broccoli and meat mixture between four airtight containers; keep in your refrigerator for up to 3 to 4 days.
For freezing, place the broccoli and meat mixture in airtight containers or heavy-duty freezer bags. Freeze up to 2 to 3 months. Defrost in the refrigerator. Bon appétit!

95. Finger-Lickin' Good Beef Brisket

Ready in about 3 hours 30 minutes
Servings 8

Delight your family with this beef brisket that's rubbed with tangy mustard, pungent garlic, and a mix of dried aromatics.

Per serving: 219 Calories; 7.2g Fat; 0.6g Carbs; 34.6g Protein; 0.1g Sugars

Ingredients

2 pounds beef brisket, trimmed
1 tablespoon Dijon mustard
2 garlic cloves, halved
1 teaspoon sea salt
1/2 teaspoon freshly ground black pepper
1 teaspoon shallot powder
1 teaspoon dried rosemary
1 teaspoon dried marjoram
1/4 cup dry red wine

Directions

- Start by preheating an oven to 375 degrees F. Rub the raw brisket with garlic and Dijon mustard.
- Then, make a dry rub by mixing the remaining ingredients. Season the brisket on both sides with the rub. Pour the wine into the pan.
- Lay beef brisket in a baking pan. Roast in the oven for 1 hour.
- Decrease the oven temperature to 300 degrees F; roast an additional 2 hours 30 minutes. Afterwards, slice the meat. Let cool completely.

Storing

Place the beef brisket along with cooking juices in airtight containers or Ziploc bags; keep in your refrigerator for 3 to 5 days.
For freezing, place the beef brisket along with cooking juices in airtight containers or heavy-duty freezer bags. Freeze up to 3 months. Defrost in the refrigerator. Enjoy!

96. Juicy Grilled Steak Medallions

Ready in about 50 minutes
Servings 4

You won't believe how fast this beef dish will be done! This is excellent served over grilled vegetables.

Per serving: 326 Calories; 11.1g Fat; 1.6g Carbs; 52g Protein; 0.2g Sugars

Ingredients

4 steak medallions, 1 1/2 inches thick
1 teaspoon sea salt
1/2 teaspoon ground black pepper
1 tablespoon cayenne pepper
1 teaspoon fennel seeds
1 teaspoon celery seeds
1/2 teaspoon chipotle powder
2 tablespoons fresh lime juice
1 tablespoon ginger root, freshly grated

Directions

- Place steak medallions in a large-sized resealable bag. Then, thoroughly combine the remaining ingredients to make the marinade.
- Marinate steak medallions for 40 minutes at room temperature.
- Preheat your grill to medium-high. Remove medallions from marinade and grill on each side to desired doneness, about 5 to 6 minutes.
- Let cool completely.

Storing

Place steak medallions in airtight containers; keep in your refrigerator for up to 3 to 4 days.
For freezing, place the steak medallions in airtight containers or heavy-duty freezer bags. Freeze up to 2 to 3 months. Defrost in the refrigerator. Bon appétit!

97. Holiday Pork and Bacon Meatloaf

Ready in about 1 hour 10 minutes
Servings 6

You don't have to make a rock-solid plan to stay on your keto diet during the holidays. It will be easy with this amazing recipe. Make this meatloaf and you'll be just fine.

Per serving: 405 Calories; 24.6g Fat; 2.8g Carbs; 40.6g Protein; 0.9g Sugars

Ingredients

1 teaspoon lard, melted
1 yellow onion, chopped
1 teaspoon garlic, finely minced
1 ¼ pounds ground pork
1 egg, beaten
2 ounces half-and-half
1 teaspoon celery seeds
Salt and ground black pepper, to taste
1/4 teaspoon cayenne pepper
1/2 pound pork sausage, broken up
1 bunch cilantro, roughly chopped
6 strips bacon

Directions

- Preheat your oven to 395 degrees F. Lightly grease a baking dish and set it aside.
- Heat the lard in a cast-iron skillet over a medium heat. Next, sauté the onions and garlic until they are tender and fragrant, for 2 to 4 minutes.
- Stir in the pork and cook until it is no longer pink, about 2 minutes.
- In a mixing bowl, thoroughly combine the egg, half-and-half, celery seeds, salt, black pepper, cayenne pepper, pork sausage and cilantro.
- Add the reserved pork mixture; stir to combine well. Lastly, shape the mixture into a loaf.
- Place the bacon on the top of your meatloaf. Bake about 1 hour. Let cool completely.

Storing

Wrap your meatloaf tightly with heavy-duty aluminum foil or plastic wrap. Then, keep in your refrigerator for up to 3 to 4 days.
For freezing, wrap your meatloaf tightly to prevent freezer burn. Freeze up to 3 to 4 months. Defrost in the refrigerator. Bon appétit!

98. Summer Baby Back Ribs

Ready in about 1 hour 40 minutes + marinating time
Servings 6

Summer is better with a barbecue! It's the perfect time to get back in shape while eating your favorite food!

Per serving: 255 Calories; 13.9g Fat; 0.8g Carbs; 29.9g Protein; 0.1g Sugars

Ingredients

1 ½ pounds baby back ribs
Salt and ground black pepper, to taste
1 teaspoon dried marjoram
1 lime, halved
1 garlic clove, minced

Directions

- Season the baby back ribs with the salt, pepper and marjoram. Now, rub your ribs with the cut sides of lime.
- Cover and transfer to your refrigerator for 6 hours. Place the minced garlic on top of the ribs.
- Grill for about 1 hour 30 minutes, turning twice to ensure even cooking.

Storing

Divide ribs into six portions. Place each portion of ribs in an airtight container; keep in your refrigerator for 3 to 5 days.
For freezing, place the ribs in airtight containers or heavy-duty freezer bags. Freeze up to 4 to 6 months. Defrost in the refrigerator. Bon appétit!

99. Slow Cooker Cajun Beef Brisket and Veggies

Ready in about 6 hours + marinating time
Servings 6

Marinated and seasoned beef brisket goes wonderfully with slow-cooked vegetables. Trim the fat off beef brisket before slow cooking.

Per serving: 296 Calories; 12g Fat; 7g Carbs; 35.2g Protein; 3.8g Sugars

Ingredients

1 ½ pounds beef brisket
1 teaspoon garlic, smashed
Ground black pepper, to taste
1 tablespoon Cajun seasonings
2 tablespoons dry red wine
2 tablespoons Worcestershire sauce
2 tablespoons vegetable oil
2 yellow onions, sliced into half moons
2 carrots, sliced
2 celery stalks, chopped
1 cup stock

Directions

- Rub beef brisket with garlic, black pepper and Cajun seasonings. Add the wine, Worcestershire sauce and 1 tablespoon of vegetable oil.
- Wrap with foil and place in the refrigerator for 3 hours.
- Heat 1 tablespoon of vegetable oil in your slow cooker. Now, sauté the onions until just tender.
- In a pan, sear the brisket until it has a golden brown crust. Transfer to your slow cooker. Add the carrots, celery and stock
- Cover and cook on Low heat setting for 6 hours or until the beef brisket is as soft as you want it. Let cool completely.

Storing

Place the beef brisket along with vegetables in airtight containers or Ziploc bags; keep in your refrigerator for 3 to 5 days.
For freezing, place the beef brisket along with vegetables in airtight containers or heavy-duty freezer bags. Freeze up to 3 months. Defrost in the refrigerator. Bon appétit!

100. Dinner Party Pork Gumbo

Ready in about 35 minutes
Servings 6

Everyone loves a good and rich gumbo! For the Keto version, just skip French cooking roux and use flaxseed meal instead.

Per serving: 427 Calories; 26.2g Fat; 13.6g Carbs; 35.2g Protein; 3.3g Sugars

Ingredients

2 tablespoons olive oil
1 pound pork shoulder, cubed
8 ounces pork sausage, sliced
2 shallots, toughly chopped
1 teaspoon beef bouillon granules
Sea salt and freshly cracked black pepper
1 teaspoon gumbo file
1 teaspoon crushed red pepper
1 tablespoon Cajun spice
4 cups bone broth
1 cup water
2 bell peppers, deveined and thinly sliced
2 celery stalks, chopped
1/4 cup flaxseed meal
3/4 pound okra

Directions

- Heat the oil in a heavy-bottomed pot that is preheated over a moderately high flame. Now, cook the pork until it is just browned; reserve.
- Add the sausage and cook in pan drippings approximately 5 minutes; reserve.
- Stir in the shallots and cook until they are softened. Add beef bouillon granules, salt, pepper, gumbo file, red pepper, Cajun spice and bone broth. Bring it to a boil.
- Add the water, bell pepper and celery, and reduce the heat to medium-low. Cook an additional 15 to 23 minutes.
- Afterwards, stir in the flax seed meal and okra; cook for a further 5 minutes or until heated through. Let cool completely.

Storing

Spoon your gumbo into three airtight containers; keep in your refrigerator for up to 3 to 4 days.
For freezing, place it in airtight containers or heavy-duty freezer bags. It will maintain the best quality for about 5 months. Defrost in the refrigerator. Enjoy!

101. Carrot and Meat Loaf Muffins

Ready in about 35 minutes
Servings 6

Meatloaf muffins are super cute and incredibly delicious. It's a great idea for a kid's birthday party!

Per serving: 220 Calories; 6.3g Fat; 5.4g Carbs; 33.8g Protein; 2.9g Sugars

Ingredients

1 pound pork, ground
1/2 pound turkey, ground
1 cup carrots, shredded
2 ripe tomatoes, pureed
1 ounce envelope onion soup mix
1 tablespoon Worcestershire sauce
1 tablespoon Dijon mustard
1/2 teaspoon dry basil
1 teaspoon dry oregano
Kosher salt and ground black pepper, to taste
2 cloves of garlic, minced
1 eggs, whisked
1 cup mozzarella cheese, shredded

Directions

- Start by preheating your oven to 350 degrees F.
- Then, thoroughly combine all ingredients until everything is blended.
- Spoon the mixture into a muffin tin that is previously coated with a nonstick cooking spray.
- Bake for 30 minutes; allow them to cool slightly before removing from the tin.

Storing

Wrap the meatloaf muffins tightly with heavy-duty aluminum foil or plastic wrap. Then, keep in your refrigerator for up to 3 to 4 days.
For freezing, wrap the meatloaf muffins tightly to prevent freezer burn. Freeze up to 3 to 4 months. Defrost in the refrigerator. Bon appétit!

102. Tomato Rum-Glazed Chicken Thighs

Ready in about 1 hour + marinating time
Servings 4

Is there anything better than glazed chicken thighs during autumn weeknights? Rum, tomato and chicken go hand in hand so you will love these boozy wings.

Per serving: 307 Calories; 12.1g Fat; 2.7g Carbs; 33.6g Protein; 1g Sugars

Ingredients

2 pounds chicken thighs
2 tablespoons olive oil
Sea salt and ground black pepper, to taste
1 teaspoon paprika
1 teaspoon dried oregano
1 teaspoon dried marjoram
2 ripe tomatoes, pureed
3/4 cup dark rum
3 tablespoons soy sauce
2 tablespoons Swerve
2 habanero chile peppers, minced
1 tablespoon minced fresh ginger
1 teaspoon ground allspice
2 tablespoons fresh lime juice, plus wedges for serving

Directions

- Start by preheating your oven to 420 degrees F.
- Now, toss chicken thighs with olive oil, salt, black pepper, paprika, oregano, and marjoram.
- In a separate mixing bowl, thoroughly combine pureed tomato puree, rum, soy sauce, Swerve, habanero peppers, ginger, allspice and fresh lime juice.
- Pour the rum/tomato mixture over chicken thighs and refrigerate, covered, for 2 hours.
- Discard the marinade and arrange chicken thighs on a rimmed baking pan. Bake for 50 minutes or until thoroughly cooked.
- In the meantime, cook the reserved marinade in a pan over a moderate heat; continue to cook until the liquid has reduced by half.
- Pour the sauce over the chicken thighs and place under the broiler for 4 minutes on high. Let cool completely.

Storing

Place chicken thighs in airtight containers or Ziploc bags; keep in your refrigerator for up 3 to 4 days.
For freezing, place them in airtight containers or heavy-duty freezer bags. Freeze up to 3 months. Once thawed in the refrigerator, heat in the preheated oven at 375 degrees F for 20 to 25 minutes or until heated through. Enjoy!

103. Oven Fried Crispy Chicken Legs

Ready in about 50 minutes
Servings 4

Here's a ridiculously simple trick to make crispy chicken legs that are tender and juicy on the inside. Just keep reading the recipe.

Per serving: 345 Calories; 14.1g Fat; 0.4g Carbs; 50.8g Protein; 0g Sugars

Ingredients

4 chicken legs
1 tablespoon butter
1 teaspoon bouillon powder
1/4 teaspoon ground black pepper, or more to the taste
Salt, to your liking
1 teaspoon paprika
1 teaspoon dried basil
1 teaspoon dried rosemary

Directions

- Start by preheating an oven to 420 degrees F. Line a rimmed baking sheet with a piece of parchment paper.
- Next, air-dry chicken legs and rub them with the butter. Then, sprinkle the chicken with all remaining ingredients.
- Arrange chicken legs out in a single layer on the prepared baking sheet.
- Bake chicken legs until skin is crispy, about 45 minutes. Let cool completely.

Storing

Divide chicken legs between four airtight containers; keep in your refrigerator for up 3 to 4 days.
For freezing, place them in airtight containers or heavy-duty freezer bags. Freeze up to 3 months. Defrost in the refrigerator. Enjoy!

104. Spicy Chicken with Brussels Sprouts

Ready in about 20 minutes
Servings 4

Have you missed spicy chicken breasts? Try this recipe and enjoy unexpected aromas and flavors! The star of this dish is chipotle chile powder that will give a smoky flavor and spiciness to the entire meal.

Per serving: 273 Calories; 15.4g Fat; 12.2g Carbs; 23g Protein; 3.1g Sugars

Ingredients

2 tablespoons sesame oil
1 ½ pounds Brussels sprouts, trimmed and cut into halves
1/4 teaspoon seasoned salt
2 cloves garlic, minced
3/4 pound chicken breasts, chopped into bite-sized pieces
1/2 cup white onions, chopped
1 cup bone broth, low-sodium
2 tablespoons Sauvignon wine
1/2 teaspoon chipotle chile powder
1/2 teaspoon whole black peppercorns
2 tablespoons fresh chives, chopped

Directions

- Heat 1 tablespoon of oil in a pan over a moderate heat. Now, sauté the Brussels sprouts for 2 to 4 minutes or until golden brown. Season with salt; reserve.
- Heat remaining 1 tablespoon of oil in the same pan that is preheated over moderately high heat Add the garlic and chicken; cook about 3 minutes.
- Add the onions, broth, wine, chipotle chile powder, and black peppercorns. Bring to a boil and reduce the heat to a simmer. Simmer for 4 minutes more.
- Add the reserved Brussels sprouts to the pan and garnish with fresh chopped chives. Let cool completely.

Storing

Place chicken breasts along with Brussels sprouts in airtight containers or Ziploc bags; keep in your refrigerator for 3 to 4 days.
For freezing, place them in airtight containers or heavy-duty freezer bags. It will maintain the best quality for about 4 months. Defrost in the refrigerator. Enjoy!

105. Vodka Duck Fillets

Ready in about 20 minutes
Servings 4

You will love this super-easy poultry dinner. It is extremely delicious and fulfilled, and it takes under 20 minutes to make.

Per serving: 351 Calories; 24.7g Fat; 9.6g Carbs; 22.1g Protein; 4.6g Sugars

Ingredients

1 tablespoon lard, room temperature
4 duck fillets
4 green onions, white and green parts, chopped
Salt and cayenne pepper, to taste
1 teaspoon mixed peppercorns
1 ½ cups turkey stock
3 tablespoons Worcestershire sauce
2 ounces vodka
1/2 teaspoon ground bay leaf
1/2 cup sour cream

Directions

- Melt the lard in a skillet that is preheated over medium-high heat. Sear duck fillets, turning once, for 4 to 6 minutes.
- Now, add the remaining ingredients, except for the sour cream, to the skillet. Cook, partially covered, for a further 7 minutes.
- Garnish with sour cream. Let cool completely.

Storing

Place duck fillets in airtight containers or Ziploc bags; keep in your refrigerator for up to 3 to 4 days.
For freezing, place them in airtight containers or heavy-duty freezer bags. Freeze up to 2 to 3 months. Once thawed in the refrigerator, reheat them in a saucepan. Bon appétit!

106. Holiday Turkey Wrapped in Prosciutto

Ready in about 30 minutes
Servings 5

You don't need to be an expert chef to make this tasty, gourmet turkey dish. Your guests will be delighted!

Per serving: 286 Calories; 9.7g Fat; 7.9g Carbs; 39.9g Protein; 5.4g Sugars

Ingredients

2 pounds turkey breasts, marinated
1 ½ tablespoons coconut butter, room temperature
1 teaspoon cayenne pepper
1/2 teaspoon chili powder
1 sprig rosemary, finely chopped
2 sprigs fresh thyme, finely chopped
2 tablespoons Cabernet Sauvignon
1 teaspoon garlic, finely minced
1 teaspoon sea salt
1/2 teaspoon freshly ground black pepper
10 strips prosciutto

Directions

- Cut the turkey breasts into 10 even slices.
- Melt the coconut butter in a nonstick skillet over a moderate heat. Sear the turkey breasts for 2 to 3 minutes on each side.
- Sprinkle turkey breasts with all seasonings and minced garlic; drizzle with wine. Now, wrap each turkey piece into one prosciutto strip.
- Preheat your oven to 450 degrees F. Lay the wrapped turkey in a roasting pan; roast about 25 minutes. Let cool completely.

Storing

Wrap the turkey pieces in foil before packing them into airtight containers; keep in your refrigerator for up to 3 to 4 days.
For freezing, place them in airtight containers or heavy-duty freezer bags. Freeze up to 2 to 3 months. Defrost in the refrigerator. Bon appétit!

107. Crock Pot Spare Ribs

Ready in about 4 hours 30 minutes
Servings 4

You can totally rely on this foolproof pork recipe and make it for any family gathering! In addition, these spare ribs are surprisingly easy to make!

Per serving: 412 Calories; 22g Fat; 3g Carbs; 46.3g Protein; 1g Sugars

Ingredients

1 tablespoon lard, at room temperature
1 ½ pounds spare ribs
3/4 cup vegetable stock, preferably homemade
2 teaspoons Swerve
2 cloves garlic, chopped
1 Serrano pepper, chopped
A bunch of scallions, chopped
Salt, to taste
1/2 teaspoon ground cumin
1 teaspoon whole black peppercorns
2 bay leaves

Directions

- Melt the lard in a pan over a moderately high heat. Cook spare ribs for 8 minutes, turning occasionally.
- In the meantime, whisk the stock, Swerve, garlic, Serrano pepper, scallions, salt and cumin in a mixing dish.
- Transfer browned spare ribs to your crock pot; pour in the stock mixture. Add black peppercorns and bay leaves.
- Cook for 4 hours 30 minutes on Low heat setting. Let cool completely.

Storing

Divide ribs into four portions. Place each portion of ribs along with roasted peppers in an airtight container; keep in your refrigerator for 3 to 5 days.
For freezing, place the ribs in airtight containers or heavy-duty freezer bags. Freeze up to 4 to 6 months. Defrost in the refrigerator. Reheat in your oven at 250 degrees F until heated through. Bon appétit!

108. Sage and Milk Pork Loin

Ready in about 1 hour 35 minutes
Servings 8

Looking for a delicious and satisfying family dish? Pork loin roast is one of the most convenient meat dishes that cooks perfectly in the oven. This time, we will add the milk for even juicier and more flavorful pork loin.

Per serving: 293 Calories; 15.4g Fat; 5.4g Carbs; 31.4g Protein; 4.4g Sugars

Ingredients

3 teaspoons olive oil
2 pounds pork loin
Salt and cayenne pepper, to taste
1 teaspoon dried thyme
1/2 cup shallots, sliced
2 bell peppers, deveined and thinly sliced
2 cup full-fat milk
1 tablespoon dried sage, crushed

Directions

- Start by preheating your oven to 330 degrees F.
- Heat the oil in a pan over a moderate flame. Sear the pork loin in a pan until just browned.
- Transfer the loin to a baking pan. Season with salt, pepper, and thyme. Scatter sliced shallot and peppers around the meat.
- Pour in the milk and cover the pan tightly with a piece of foil. Roast for 1 hour 30 minutes, turning the loin once or twice.
- Carve the pork loin and transfer to a serving plate along with roasted vegetables as well as cooking liquid. Garnish with sage leaves. Let cool completely.

Storing

Divide the pork loin and vegetables between two airtight containers; keep in your refrigerator for 3 to 5 days.
For freezing, place the pork loin and vegetables in airtight containers or heavy-duty freezer bags. Freeze up to 4 to 6 months. Defrost in the refrigerator.

109. Easy Aromatic Pork Chops

Ready in about 30 minutes
Servings 4

For this delicious pork recipe, use a decent quality drinking wine like Pinot gris, Sauvignon blanc or Semillons. You can skip the wine by substituting it with chicken broth and water (in the same proportion) + Dijon mustard to taste.

Per serving: 335 Calories; 26.3g Fat; 2.5g Carbs; 18.3g Protein; 0.8g Sugars

Ingredients

2 tablespoons lard, melted
1/2 cup red onion, thinly sliced
3 cloves garlic, minced
4 pork chops
1/4 cup dry white wine
2 tablespoons Worcestershire sauce
1 teaspoon dried thyme
4 allspice berries, lightly crushed
1/2 teaspoon fresh ginger root, grated

Directions

- Melt the lard in a saucepan over medium heat. Sauté the onions and garlic until aromatic and just browned.
- Add the pork and cook 15 to 20 minutes, turning once or twice. Add dry white wine, Worcestershire sauce, thyme, crushed allspice berries and fresh ginger.
- Cook an additional 8 minutes or until everything is thoroughly heated. Let cool completely.

Storing

Place pork chops and sauce in airtight containers or Ziploc bags; keep in your refrigerator for 3 to 4 days. Freeze the pork chops in sauce in airtight containers or heavy-duty freezer bags. Freeze up to 4 months. Defrost in the refrigerator. Bon appétit!

110. Super Crispy Roasted Pork Shoulder

Ready in about 25 minutes
Servings 4

Pork shoulder is probably one of the most convenient and versatile foods to cook under the broiler. Adding a freshly grated Asiago cheese will complete your meal.

Per serving: 476 Calories; 35.3g Fat; 6.2g Carbs; 31.1g Protein; 1.2g Sugars

Ingredients

1 pound pork shoulder, cut into 1-inch-thick pieces
Salt and cayenne pepper, to taste
2 tablespoons lard
2 shallots, sliced
2 cloves garlic, smashed
1 thyme sprig
1 rosemary sprig
1 tablespoon tamarind paste
1 tablespoon fish sauce
2 tablespoons Kalamata olives, pitted and sliced
2 tablespoons rice vinegar
1 cup bone broth
1/2 cup Asiago cheese, freshly grated

Directions

- Start by preheating your broiler. Sprinkle your pork with salt and cayenne pepper on all sides.
- Melt the lard in a pan that is preheated over a moderately high flame. Sweat the shallots and garlic for about 5 minutes; reserve.
- Warm the remaining 1 tablespoon of lard. Sear the pork for 7 to 8 minutes, turning once; reserve.
- Now, cook the garlic, thyme, rosemary, tamarind paste, fish sauce, olives, vinegar, and bone broth in pan drippings. Cook until the sauce is reduced by about half. Transfer to an oven-safe dish.
- Add the reserved pork along with the shallot mixture; sprinkle with grated Asiago cheese. Lastly, broil until everything is thoroughly heated, about 5 minutes. Let cool completely.

Storing

Place the pork pieces into four airtight containers or Ziploc bags; keep in your refrigerator for 3 to 4 days. For freezing, wrap tightly with heavy-duty aluminum foil or freezer wrap. It will maintain the best quality for 2 to 3 months. Defrost in the refrigerator. Enjoy!

111. Ground Pork and Swiss Chard Skillet

Ready in about 25 minutes
Servings 4

Are you craving a burger? Try this homey dish with ground pork and you won't miss a burger bun!

Per serving: 349 Calories; 13g Fat; 8.4g Carbs; 45.3g Protein; 3.5g Sugars

Ingredients

2 tablespoons vegetable oil
2 cloves garlic, pressed
1 cup leeks, sliced
1 Serrano pepper, sliced
1 bell pepper, chopped
1 ½ pounds ground pork
1 teaspoon sea salt
1/4 teaspoon lemon pepper, or more to taste
1/4 cup tomato puree
1/4 cup dry sherry wine
1 bunch Swiss chard, trimmed and roughly chopped
1 cup beef bone broth

Directions

- Heat 1 tablespoon of vegetable oil in a pan over a moderately high heat. Now, sauté the garlic, leeks, and peppers until they are just softened; reserve.
- Heat the remaining tablespoon of vegetable oil; add the ground pork and cook, stirring frequently, for 3 to 4 minutes more.
- Add the remaining ingredients along with sautéed vegetables. Cook, covered, an additional 10 minutes or until everything is thoroughly cooked.
- Uncover and cook for a further 5 minute or until the liquid has evaporated. Let cool completely.

Storing

Place the ground pork mixture in airtight containers or Ziploc bags; keep in your refrigerator for up to 3 to 4 days.
For freezing, place it in airtight containers or heavy-duty freezer bags. Freeze up to 2 to 3 months. Defrost in the refrigerator. Bon appétit!

112. Easy and Yummy Chicken Drumettes

Ready in about 30 minutes
Servings 4

Give your chicken drumettes a simple but delicious makeover. Adding melted tallow and turkey stock makes all the difference.

Per serving: 165 Calories; 9.8g Fat; 7.7g Carbs; 12.4g Protein; 3.9g Sugars

Ingredients

2 tablespoons tallow
4 chicken drumettes
Salt, to taste
1/2 cup leeks, chopped
1 carrot, sliced
2 cloves garlic, minced
1 teaspoon cayenne pepper
1 teaspoon dried marjoram
1/2 teaspoon mustard seeds
1 cup turkey stock
2 tomatoes, crushed
1 tablespoon Worcestershire sauce
1 teaspoon mixed peppercorns
1 thyme sprig
1 rosemary sprig

Directions

- Melt the tallow in a saucepan over medium-high heat. Sprinkle the chicken drumettes with the salt.
- Then, fry the chicken drumettes until they are no longer pink and lightly browned on all sides; reserve.
- Now, cook the leeks, carrots and garlic in pan drippings over medium heat for 4 to 6 minutes.
- Reduce the heat to simmer, and add the remaining ingredients along with the reserved chicken. Simmer, partially covered, for 15 to 20 minutes. Let cool completely.

Storing

Place chicken drumettes in airtight containers or Ziploc bags; keep in your refrigerator for up 3 to 4 days.
For freezing, place them in airtight containers or heavy-duty freezer bags. Freeze up to 3 months. Once thawed in the refrigerator, heat in the preheated oven at 375 degrees F for 20 to 25 minutes or until heated through. Enjoy!

113. Ground Chicken with Peppers and Asiago Cheese

Ready in about 15 minutes
Servings 4

You'll be making this easy chicken dish on repeat all year long. Use the peppers of different colors to make an interesting and kid-friendly skillet.

Per serving: 301 Calories; 11.4g Fat; 10.2g Carbs; 37.9g Protein; 0.2g Sugars

Ingredients

1 tablespoon olive oil
1 teaspoon garlic, minced
1 cup shallots, chopped
1 chili pepper, deveined and chopped
4 bell peppers, deveined and chopped
1 pound chicken, ground
1/3 cup dry sherry
1 teaspoon Italian seasonings
Salt and black pepper, to taste
1/2 cup Asiago cheese, shredded

Directions

- Heat the oil in a pan that is preheated over a moderate flame. Now, sauté the garlic and shallots until they are aromatic.
- Now, stir in the peppers and ground chicken; cook until the chicken is no longer pink.
- Add sherry, Italian seasonings, salt and pepper. Cook an additional 5 minutes or until everything is thoroughly heated.
- Scatter Asiago cheese over the top and remove from heat. Let cool completely.

Storing

Place the ground chicken mixture in airtight containers or Ziploc bags; keep in your refrigerator for up to 3 to 4 days.
For freezing, place it in airtight containers or heavy-duty freezer bags. Freeze up to 2 to 3 months. Defrost in the refrigerator. Bon appétit!

114. Easy Herby Turkey Drumsticks

Ready in about 1 hour
Servings 2

Turkey drumsticks are delicious and so fun to eat! A marinade will give a great flavor and keep turkey meat juicy, making it buttery tender on the grill.

Per serving: 488 Calories; 24.5g Fat; 2.1g Carbs; 33.6g Protein; 0.5g Sugars

Ingredients

2 tablespoons apple cider vinegar
2 thyme sprigs, chopped
2 rosemary sprigs, chopped
1 teaspoon dried marjoram
1 teaspoon dried basil
1 teaspoon granulated garlic
2 tablespoons olive oil
2 turkey drumsticks
Salt and black pepper, to taste

Directions

- To make the marinade, thoroughly combine apple cider vinegar, thyme, rosemary, marjoram, basil, granulated garlic, and olive oil in a mixing bowl.
- Now, marinate the turkey at least 3 hours in the refrigerator.
- Cook turkey drumsticks on a preheated grill for 45 minutes to 1 hour or until a meat thermometer has reached the temperature of 180 degrees F. Season with salt and pepper to taste. Let cool completely.

Storing

Wrap the turkey drumsticks in foil before packing them into an airtight container; keep in your refrigerator for up to 3 to 4 days.
For freezing, place them in airtight containers or heavy-duty freezer bags. Freeze up to 2 to 3 months. Defrost in the refrigerator. Bon appétit!

115. Pork Quiche with Bell Peppers

Ready in about 50 minutes
Servings 6

Sometimes a true comfort food such pork quiche and a cup of yoghurt is all you really need. Whether it is a family lunch or celebratory dinner, pork quiche is always a great idea!

Per serving: 478 Calories; 36g Fat; 4.9g Carbs; 33.5g Protein; 1.4g Sugars

Ingredients

6 eggs, lightly beaten
2 ½ cups almond flour
1 stick butter, melted
1 ¼ pounds ground pork
Salt and pepper, to the taste
1 green bell pepper, thinly sliced
1 red bell pepper, thinly sliced
1 cup heavy cream
1/2 teaspoon mustard seeds
1/2 teaspoon dried dill weed

Directions

- Start by preheating your oven to 350 degrees F
- Add an egg, flour, and butter to a mixing dish; mix to combine well.
- Press the batter dough in a baking pan that is previously greased with a nonstick cooking spray.
- Next, brown ground pork for 3 to 5 minutes, crumbling with a wide spatula; season with salt and pepper.
- In another mixing bowl, thoroughly combine the remaining ingredients; add browned pork.
- Spread this mixture over the crust and bake for 35 to 43 minutes in the preheated oven. Transfer to a wire rack to cool before slicing.

Storing

Slice the quiche into six pieces; divide between airtight containers or Ziploc bags; keep in your refrigerator for up to 3 days.
For freezing, place them in airtight containers or heavy-duty freezer bags. Freeze up to 3 months. Once thawed in the refrigerator, heat in the microwave until warmed through. Enjoy!

116. Crock Pot Hungarian Goulash

Ready in about 10 hours
Servings 4

Traditional Hungarian goulash is the perfect for a keto dinner! If you used to serve hot cooked rice on the side, just swap it for a cauliflower rice. It will surprise you with its taste!

Per serving: 517 Calories; 35.7g Fat; 10.7g Carbs; 38.2g Protein; 4g Sugars

Ingredients

1 ½ tablespoons butter
1 pound pork shoulder off the bone, chopped
1 cup yellow onions, chopped
3 garlic cloves, crushed
2 teaspoons cayenne pepper
1 teaspoon sweet Hungarian paprika
1 teaspoon caráway seeds, ground
4 cups chicken stock
2 ½ cups tomato puree
2 chili peppers, deveined and finely chopped
For the Sour Cream Sauce:
1 cup sour cream
1 bunch parsley, chopped
1 teaspoon lemon zest

Directions

- Melt the butter in a sauté pan that is preheated over a moderate heat. Now, cook the pork until just browned; reserve.
- Add the onions and garlic and continue to sauté until they are just tender and fragrant.
- Transfer reserved pork along with the onions and garlic to your crock pot. Add the cayenne pepper, paprika, caraway seeds, stock, tomato puree and chili peppers.
- Cover and cook for 8 to 10 hours on low heat setting.
- In the meantime, make the sour cream sauce by whisking all the sauce ingredients. Let cool completely.

Storing

Spoon goulash into four airtight containers or Ziploc bags; keep in your refrigerator for up to 3 to 4 days.
For freezing, place the goulash in airtight containers. Freeze up to 4 to 6 months. Defrost in the refrigerator.
Place the sour cream sauce in an airtight glass jar; keep in your refrigerator for up to 2 to 3 days. Bon appétit!

117. Moms' Aromatic Fish Curry

Ready in about 25 minutes
Servings 6

This amazing curry combines fresh fish with curry leaves, cardamom pods, garlic and coconut milk, plus flavor-building ingredients like coriander and ginger.

Per serving: 270 Calories; 16.9g Fat; 8.6g Carbs; 22.3g Protein; 2.2g Sugars

Ingredients

2 tablespoons fresh lime juice
2 pounds blue grenadier, cut into large pieces
2 tablespoons olive oil
8 fresh curry leaves
1 cup shallots, chopped
2 green chilies, minced
1/2 tablespoon fresh ginger, grated
2 garlic cloves, finely chopped
2 green cardamom pods
1 teaspoon dried basil
Salt and black pepper, to taste
4 Roma tomatoes, pureed
1 tablespoon ground coriander
1 cup coconut milk

Directions

- Drizzle blue grenadier with lime juice.
- Heat the oil in a nonstick skillet over a moderate flame. Cook curry leaves and shallots until the shallot is softened, about 4 minutes.
- After that, add the chilies, ginger and garlic and cook an additional minute or until fragrant. Add the remaining ingredients, except for coconut milk, and simmer for 10 minutes or until heated through.
- Now, stir in the fish; pour in 1 cup of coconut milk and cook, covered, for 6 minutes longer. Let cool completely.

Storing

Spoon fish curry into three airtight containers; it will last for 3 to 4 days in the refrigerator.
For freezing, place fish curry in airtight containers or heavy-duty freezer bags. Freeze up to 4 to 6 months. Defrost in the microwave or refrigerator. Bon appétit!

118. Mackerel Steak Casserole with Cheese and Veggies

Ready in about 30 minutes
Servings 4

Fresh-from-the-sea fish steaks are a great family meal for any occasion. This rich and flavorful casserole is simply delicious and it is ready in 30 minutes.

Per serving: 301 Calories; 14g Fat; 10g Carbs; 33.3g Protein; 3.3g Sugars

Ingredients

1/2 stick butter
1 cup carrots, thinly sliced
1 cup parsnip, thinly sliced
2 cloves garlic, thinly sliced
2 onions, thinly sliced
1/4 cup clam juice
3 tomatoes, thinly sliced
1 pound mackerel steaks
1 tablespoon Old Bay seasoning
Salt and black pepper, to your liking
1 cup mozzarella, shredded
1/2 cup fresh chives, chopped

Directions

- Preheat your oven to 450 degrees F.
- Melt the butter in a pan that is previously preheated over a moderate flame. Cook the carrots, parsnip, garlic, and onions until they are tender.
- Add clam juice and tomatoes and cook 4 minutes more. Transfer this vegetable mixture to a casserole dish.
- Lay the fish steaks on top of the vegetable layer. Sprinkle with seasonings. Cover with foil and roast for 10 minutes, until the fish is opaque in the center.
- Top with shredded cheese and bake another 5 minutes. Garnish with fresh chopped chives. Let cool completely.

Storing

Slice the casserole into four pieces. Divide the pieces into four airtight containers; it will last for 3 to 4 days in the refrigerator.
For freezing, place each portion in a separate heavy-duty freezer bag. Freeze up to 2 to 3 months. Defrost in the microwave or refrigerator. Bon appétit!

119. Grilled Clams with Tomato Sauce

Ready in about 25 minutes
Servings 4

Clams are plentiful, flavorful and easy to cook. Tangy tomato sauce is classic with clams. Enjoy!

Per serving: 134 Calories; 7.8g Fat; 7.9g Carbs; 8.3g Protein; 3.2g Sugars

Ingredients

40 littleneck clams
For the Sauce:
2 tablespoons olive oil
1 onion, chopped
1 teaspoon crushed garlic
2 tomatoes, pureed
Sea salt and freshly ground black pepper, to taste
1/2 teaspoon cayenne pepper
1/3 cup dry sherry
1 lemon, cut into wedges

Directions

- Heat grill to medium-high. Cook until clams open, about 6 minutes.
- Heat the oil in sauté pan over a moderate heat. Cook the onion and garlic until aromatic.
- Add pureed tomatoes, salt, black pepper and cayenne pepper and cook an additional 10 minutes or until everything is thoroughly cooked.
- Remove from heat and add dry sherry; stir to combine. Add grilled clams and lemon wedges. Let cool completely.

Storing

Spoon clams with sauce into four airtight containers; it will last for 3 to 4 days in the refrigerator.
For freezing, place clams along with sauce in airtight containers or heavy-duty freezer bags. Freeze up to 3 months. Defrost in your refrigerator. Bon appétit!

120. Seafood and Andouille Medley

Ready in about 25 minutes
Servings 4

Is there anything better than rich, warm medley during winter weekdays? Serve with a sour cream on the side for a full keto experience.

Per serving: 481 Calories; 26.9g Fat; 10g Carbs; 46.6g Protein; 1.1g Sugars

Ingredients

1/2 stick butter, melted
2 andouille sausages, cut crosswise into 1/2-inch-thick slices
2 garlic cloves, finely minced
1 shallot, chopped
2 tomatoes, pureed
1 tablespoon oyster sauce
3/4 cup clam juice
1/3 cup dry white wine
1/2 pound skinned sole, cut into chunks
20 sea scallops
2 tablespoons fresh cilantro, chopped

Directions

- Melt the butter in a heavy-bottomed pot over medium-high heat. Cook the sausages until no longer pink; reserve.
- Now, sauté the garlic and shallots in pan drippings until they are softened; reserve.
- Add the pureed tomatoes, oyster sauce, clam juice and wine; simmer for another 12 minutes.
- Add the skinned sole, scallops and reserved sausages. Let it simmer, partially covered, for 6 minutes. Garnished with fresh cilantro. Let cool completely.

Storing

Spoon the medley into an airtight container; keep in your refrigerator for 3 to 4 days.
For freezing, place the medley in airtight containers or heavy-duty freezer bags. Freeze up to 3 months. Defrost in the microwave. Bon appétit!

VEGAN

121. Sunday Stuffed Mushrooms

Ready in about 30 minutes
Servings 4

If you crave stuffed vegetables, nothing could be easier than filling mushroom caps with a tasty nutty stuffing and bake them in the preheated oven.

Per serving: 139 Calories; 11.2g Fat; 7.4g Carbs; 4.8g Protein; 3.6g Sugars

Ingredients

2 tablespoons sesame oil
1 cup onions, chopped
1 garlic clove, minced
1 pound white mushrooms, stems removed
Salt and black pepper, to taste
1/4 cup raw walnuts, crushed
2 tablespoons cilantro, chopped

Directions

- Begin by preheating an oven to 360 degrees F. Lightly grease a large baking sheet with a nonstick cooking spray.
- Heat sesame oil in a frying pan that is preheated over medium-high heat. Now, sauté the onions and garlic until aromatic.
- Then, chop the mushroom stems and cook until they are tender. Heat off, season with salt and pepper; stir in walnuts.
- Stuff the mushroom caps with walnut/mushroom mixture and arrange them on the prepared baking sheet.
- Bake for 25 minutes and transfer to a wire rack to cool slightly. Garnish with fresh cilantro. Let cool completely.

Storing

Place stuffed mushrooms in airtight containers; keep in your refrigerator for 3 to 5 days.
Place stuffed mushrooms on the parchment-lined baking sheet, about 1-inch apart from each other; freezer for about 2 to 3 hours.
Remove frozen mushrooms to a plastic freezer bag for long-term storage; they will maintain the best quality for 10 to 12 months.

122. Rich Dark Chocolate Smoothie

Ready in about 10 minutes
Servings 2

The incredible combination of nuts, cocoa and seeds is fitting for breakfast or a snack. Once you taste how good this smoothie is, it will become your ketogenic breakfast staple.

Per serving: 335 Calories; 31.7g Fat; 12.7g Carbs; 7g Protein; 4.9g Sugars

Ingredients

8 walnuts
3/4 cup almond milk
1/4 cup water
1 ½ cups lettuce
2 teaspoons vegan protein powder, zero carbs
1 tablespoon chia seeds
1 tablespoon unsweetened cocoa powder
4 fresh dates, pitted

Directions

- Process all ingredients in your blender until everything is uniform and creamy.

Storing

Pour the prepared smoothie into two glass containers with airtight lids; make sure to fill the containers to the very top. Seal your containers tightly and store in the refrigerator for up to 24 hours.
To freeze, pour the smoothie into freezer-safe jars. They will maintain the best quality for 3 months. Defrost in your refrigerator overnight. Once defrosted, just stir enjoy!

123. Roasted Asparagus with Baba Ghanoush

Ready in about 45 minutes
Servings 6

The eggplant season is a great time to try out this classic Middle Eastern dip! Ultimately, you need something creamy, soft and delicious to serve with timeless roasted asparagus spears.

Per serving: 149 Calories; 12.1g Fat; 9g Carbs; 3.6g Protein; 4.3g Sugars

Ingredients

1 ½ pounds asparagus spears, trim and cut off the woody ends
1/4 cup olive oil
1 teaspoon sea salt
1/2 teaspoon ground black pepper, to taste
1/2 teaspoon paprika

For Baba Ghanoush:
3/4 pound eggplant
2 teaspoons olive oil
1/2 cup scallions, chopped
2 cloves garlic, minced
1 tablespoon tahini
2 tablespoons fresh lemon juice
1/2 teaspoon cayenne pepper
Salt and ground black pepper, to taste
1/4 cup fresh parsley leaves, chopped

Directions

- Begin by preheating your oven to 390 degrees F. Line a baking sheet with parchment paper.
- Place the asparagus spears on the baking sheet.
- Toss asparagus spears with the oil, salt, pepper, and paprika. Bake about 9 minutes or until thoroughly cooked.
- Then, make Baba Ghanoush. Preheat your oven to 425 degrees F.
- Place the eggplants on a lined cookie sheet. Set under the broiler approximately 30 minutes; allow eggplants to cool. Now, peel the eggplants and remove the stems.
- Heat 2 teaspoons of olive oil in a frying pan over a moderately high flame. Now, sauté the scallions and garlic until tender and aromatic.
- Add the roasted eggplant, scallion mixture, tahini, lemon juice, cayenne pepper, salt and black pepper to your food processor. Pulse until ingredients are evenly mixed. Top with parsley.
- Let cool completely.

Storing

Place asparagus spears in airtight containers; keep in your refrigerator for 3 to 5 days.
For freezing, wrap asparagus spears tightly in several layers of plastic wrap and squeeze the air out. Place them in a freezable container; they can be frozen for 10 to 12 month.
Place the prepared Baba Ghanoush in an airtight container. Refrigerate for up to 5 days.
Chill the Baba Ghanoush until cold throughout. Transfer it to a heavy-duty freezer bag. Freeze up to 3 months. Defrost in the refrigerator. Enjoy!

124. Roasted Curried Cauliflower with Peppers

Ready in about 35 minutes
Servings 4

Roasted vegetables are a must-have for Sunday lunch or Christmas dinner. In addition, this recipe is super-easy and extremely addictive, high in fiber and vitamins but low in carbs!

Per serving: 166 Calories; 13.9g Fat; 9.4g Carbs; 3g Protein; 4.4g Sugars

Ingredients

1 pound cauliflower, broken into florets
2 bell peppers, halved
2 pasilla peppers, halved
1/4 cup extra-virgin olive oil
1/2 teaspoon sea salt
1/4 teaspoon freshly ground black pepper, or more to taste
1/2 teaspoon cayenne pepper
1 teaspoon curry powder
1/2 teaspoon nigella seeds

Directions

- Preheat your oven to 425 degrees F. Line a large baking sheet with a piece of parchment paper.
- Drizzle cauliflower and peppers with extra-virgin olive oil. Sprinkle with salt, black pepper, cayenne pepper, curry powder and nigella seeds
- Next, arrange the vegetables on the prepared baking sheet.
- Roast the vegetables, tossing periodically, until they are slightly browned, about 30 minutes. Let cool completely.

Storing

Place roasted cauliflower in airtight containers; keep in your refrigerator for 3 to 5 days.
Place roasted cauliflower in freezable containers; they will maintain the best quality for 10 to 12 months. Defrost in the refrigerator or microwave. Enjoy!

125. Tofu Stuffed Zucchini with Cashew Nuts

Ready in about 50 minutes
Servings 4

This is another recipe for stuffed vegetables, bursting with amazing flavors! These ultra delicious stuffed zucchini boats are rich, spicy, and comforting!

Per serving: 148 Calories; 10g Fat; 9.8g Carbs; 7.5g Protein; 5.5g Sugars

Ingredients

1 tablespoon olive oil
2 (12-ounce) packages firm tofu, drained and crumbled
2 garlic cloves, pressed
1/2 cup scallions, chopped
2 cups tomato puree
1/4 teaspoon turmeric
1/4 teaspoon chili powder
Sea salt and cayenne pepper, to taste
4 zucchinis, cut into halves lengthwise and scoop out the insides
1 tablespoon nutritional yeast
2 ounces cashew nuts, lightly salted and chopped

Directions

- Heat the oil in a pan that is preheated over a moderate heat; now, cook the tofu, garlic, and scallions for 4 to 6 minutes.
- Stir in 1 cup of tomato puree and scooped zucchini flesh; add all seasonings and cook an additional 6 minutes, until tofu is slightly browned.
- Next, preheat your oven to 360 degrees F.
- Divide the tofu mixture among zucchini shells. Place stuffed zucchini shells in a baking dish that is previously greased with a cooking spray. Pour in the remaining 1 cup of tomato puree.
- Bake approximately 30 minutes. Sprinkle with nutritional yeast and cashew nuts; bake an additional 5 to 6 minutes. Let cool completely.

Storing

Place stuffed zucchini in airtight containers or Ziploc bags; keep in your refrigerator for 3 to 4 days.
Wrap each zucchini tightly in several layers of plastic wrap and squeeze the air out. Place them in a freezable container; they can be frozen for up to 1 month. Bake the thawed zucchini at 200 degrees F until they are completely warm. Enjoy!

126. Brussels Sprouts with Tempeh

Ready in about 20 minutes
Servings 4

An amazingly quick dish that features vegetables and vegan protein. Add another combo of spices if desired. Enjoy!

Per serving: 179 Calories; 11.7g Fat; 12.1g Carbs; 10.5g Protein; 2g Sugars

Ingredients

2 tablespoons olive oil
2 garlic cloves, minced
1/2 cup leeks, chopped
10 ounces tempeh, crumbled
2 tablespoons water
2 tablespoons soy sauce
1 tablespoon tomato puree
1/2 pound Brussels sprouts, quartered
Sea salt and ground black pepper, to taste

Directions

- Heat the oil in a saucepan that is preheated over a moderate heat. Now, cook the garlic and leeks until tender and aromatic.
- Now, add the tempeh, water and soy sauce. Cook until the tempeh just beginning to brown, about 5 minutes.
- Stir in tomato puree and Brussels sprouts; season with salt and pepper; turn the heat to low and cook, stirring often, for about 13 minutes. Let cool completely.

Storing

Place Brussels sprout and tempeh in airtight containers or Ziploc bags; keep in your refrigerator for 3 to 5 days.
Place Brussels sprout and tempeh in freezable containers; they can be frozen for up to 3 months. Defrost in the refrigerator or microwave.

127. Garam Masala Broccoli Delight

Ready in about 15 minutes
Servings 4

Don't let this short list of ingredients fool you! They make a perfect match, trust me. Broccoli is a powerhouse of amazing nutrients like Vitamin C and K, as well as minerals and fiber.

Per serving: 100 Calories; 8.2g Fat; 4.7g Carbs; 3.7g Protein; 0.9g Sugars

Ingredients

3/4 pound broccoli, broken into florets
1/4 cup extra-virgin olive oil
Seasoned salt and ground black pepper, to taste
1 garlic clove, smashed
1 tablespoon sesame paste
1 tablespoon fresh lime juice
1/2 teaspoon Garam Masala

Directions

- Steam broccoli for 7 minutes, until it is crisp-tender but still vibrant green. Pulse in your blender or a food processor until rice-like consistency is achieved.
- Now, add the oil, salt, black paper, garlic, sesame paste, fresh lime juice and Garam Masala.
- Blend until everything is well incorporated.
- Drizzle with some extra olive oil. Let cool completely.

Storing

Divide garam masala broccoli into four portions; divide the portions between four airtight containers; keep in your refrigerator for up 3 to 5 days.
For freezing, place it in airtight containers. Freeze up to 10 to 12 months. Defrost in the refrigerator. Bon appétit!

128. Morning Protein Smoothie

Ready in about 5 minutes
Servings 4

Breakfast in less than 5 minutes! This smoothie has a beautiful color and amazing taste, a true feast for the eyes and belly.

Per serving: 247 Calories; 21.7g Fat; 14.9g Carbs; 2.6g Protein; 9g Sugars

Ingredients

1/2 cup water
1 ½ cups almond milk
1 banana, peeled and sliced
1/3 cup frozen cherries
1/3 cup fresh blueberries
1/4 teaspoon vanilla extract
1 tablespoon vegan protein powder, zero carbs

Directions

- Mix all ingredients in your blender or a smoothie maker until creamy and uniform.

Storing

Pour your smoothie into four glass containers with airtight lids; make sure to fill the containers to the very top. Seal your containers tightly and store in the refrigerator for up to 24 hours.
To freeze, pour the smoothie into freezer-safe jars. They will maintain the best quality for 3 months. Defrost in your refrigerator.

129. Roasted Cabbage with Sesame

Ready in about 45 minutes
Servings 6

Roast cabbage wedges with sesame seeds for a simple holiday side dish. Add a pinch of chili paper flakes for some extra oomph!

Per serving: 186 Calories; 17g Fat; 8g Carbs; 2.1g Protein; 4.9g Sugars

Ingredients

Nonstick cooking spray
2 pounds green cabbage, cut into wedges
1/4 cup olive oil
Coarsely salt and freshly ground black pepper, to taste
1 teaspoon sesame seeds
2 tablespoons fresh chives, chopped

Directions

- Begin by preheating your oven to 390 degrees F. Brush a rimmed baking sheet with a nonstick cooking spray.
- Add the cabbage wedges to the baking sheet. Toss with olive oil, salt, black pepper and sesame seeds.
- Roast for 40 to 45 minutes, until cabbage is softened. Top with fresh chopped chives.
- Let cool completely.

Storing

Place the roasted cabbage in airtight containers or Ziploc bags; keep in your refrigerator for 3 to 5 days. Place the roasted cabbage in freezable containers; they can be frozen for up to 10 months. Defrost in the refrigerator or microwave. Bon appétit!

130. Ethiopian Stuffed Peppers with Cauliflower Rice

Ready in about 40 minutes
Servings 4

Cauliflower rice is a staple you should have in your kitchen during a ketogenic diet. Every vegan dish is fast and cheap to pull together once you make a batch of cauliflower rice.

Per serving: 77 Calories; 4.8g Fat; 8.4g Carbs; 1.6g Protein; 3.2g Sugars

Ingredients

1 small head cauliflower
4 bell peppers
1 ½ tablespoons oil
1 onion, chopped
1 garlic cloves, minced
1 teaspoon chipotle powder
1 teaspoon Berbere
2 ripe tomatoes, pureed
Sea salt and pepper, to taste

Directions

- To make cauliflower rice, grate the cauliflower into the size of rice. Place on a kitchen towel to soak up any excess moisture.
- Next, preheat your oven to 360 degrees F. Lightly grease a casserole dish.
- Cut off the top of the bell peppers. Now, discard the seeds and core.
- Roast the peppers in a parchment lined baking pan for 18 minutes until the skin is slightly browned.
- In the meantime, heat the oil over medium-high heat. Sauté the onion and garlic until tender and fragrant.
- Add cauliflower rice, chipotle powder, and Berbere spice. Cook until the cauliflower rice is tender, about 6 minutes.
- Divide the cauliflower mixture among bell peppers. Place in the casserole dish.
- Mix the tomatoes, salt, and pepper. Pour the tomato mixture over the peppers. Bake about 10 minutes, depending on desired tenderness. Let cool completely.

Storing

Place stuffed peppers in airtight containers; keep in your refrigerator for 3 to 4 days.
Wrap each stuffed pepper tightly in several layers of plastic wrap and squeeze the air out. Place them in airtight containers; they can be frozen for up to 1 month.
Defrost in the refrigerator. Bake the thawed stuffed peppers at 200 degrees F until they are completely warm.

131. Vegan Tofu Skillet

Ready in about 25 minutes
Servings 4

This vegan meal is incredibly tasty and easy to make for dinner or brunch. Use another combo of vegetables if desired – just make sure to use low-carb veggies.

Per serving: 128 Calories; 8.3g Fat; 10g Carbs; 5.1g Protein; 4g Sugars

Ingredients

2 tablespoons olive oil
1 (14-ounce) block tofu, pressed and cubed
1 celery stalk, chopped
1 bunch scallions, chopped
1 teaspoon cayenne pepper
1 teaspoon garlic powder
2 tablespoons Worcestershire sauce
Salt and black pepper, to taste
1 pound Brussels sprouts, trimmed and quartered
1/2 teaspoon turmeric powder
1/2 teaspoon dried sill weed
1/4 teaspoon dried basil

Directions

- Heat 1 tablespoon of olive oil in a large-sized skillet over a moderately high flame. Add tofu cubes and cook, gently stirring, for 8 minutes.
- Now, add the celery and scallions; cook until they are softened, about 5 minutes
- Add cayenne pepper, garlic powder, Worcestershire sauce, salt, and pepper; continue to cook for 3 more minutes; reserve.
- Heat the remaining 1 tablespoon of oil in the same pan. Cook Brussels sprouts along with the remaining seasonings for 4 minutes.
- Add tofu mixture to Brussels sprouts. Let cool completely.

Storing

Place tofu mixture in airtight containers or Ziploc bags; keep in your refrigerator for 3 to 5 days.

132. The Best Guacamole Ever

Ready in about 10 minutes + chilling time
Servings 8

Choose ripe avocados and fresh tomatoes for this guacamole and you cannot go wrong. Don't over mash your avocados because you want a chunky sauce not smooth and squashy.

Per serving: 112 Calories; 9.9g Fat; 6.5g Carbs; 1.3g Protein; 1.4g Sugars

Ingredients

2 Haas avocados, peeled, pitted, and mashed
2 tablespoons fresh lime juice
Sea salt and ground black pepper, to taste
1/2 teaspoon cumin, ground
1 yellow onion, chopped
2 tablespoons coriander leaves, chopped
1 cup fresh tomatoes, chopped
2 garlic cloves, minced
1 red chili, deseeded and finely chopped

Directions

- In a bowl, thoroughly combine the avocados, lime juice, salt and black pepper.
- Stir in the onion, cilantro, tomatoes, and garlic; sprinkle with paprika.

Storing

Place guacamole in an airtight container or Ziploc bag; keep in your refrigerator for 2 days.
Place guacamole in freezable containers; they can be frozen for up to 3 to 4 months. Defrost in the refrigerator. Bon appétit!

133. Sautéed Fennel with Basil-Tomato Sauce

Ready in about 20 minutes
Servings 4

Fennel is among the healthiest foods in the world, it is a great source of vitamins, minerals, and fiber. Fennel can lower blood pressure, improve digestion and maintain bone health. Enjoy!

Per serving: 135 Calories; 13.6g Fat; 3g Carbs; 0.9g Protein; 1.1g Sugars

Ingredients

2 tablespoons olive oil
1 garlic clove, crushed
1 fennel, thinly sliced
1/4 cup vegetable stock
Sea salt and ground black pepper, to taste

For the Sauce:
2 tomatoes, halved
2 tablespoons extra-virgin olive oil
1/2 cup scallions, chopped
1 cloves garlic, minced
1 ancho chili, minced
1 bunch fresh basil, leaves picked
1 tablespoon fresh cilantro, roughly chopped
Sat and pepper, to taste

Directions

- Heat olive oil in a pan over a moderately high heat. Sauté the garlic for 1 to 2 minutes or until aromatic.
- Throw the slices of fennel into the pan; add vegetable stock and continue to cook until the fennel is softened. Season with salt and black pepper to taste. Heat off.
- Brush the tomato halves with extra-virgin olive oil. Microwave for 15 minutes on HIGH; be sure to pour off any excess liquid.
- Transfer cooked tomatoes to a food processor; add the remaining ingredients for the sauce. Puree until your desired consistency is reached. Let cool completely.

Storing

Divide sautéed fennel along with sauce into four portions; divide the portions between four airtight containers; keep in your refrigerator for up 3 to 5 days. For freezing, place it in airtight containers. Freeze up to 10 to 12 months. Defrost in the refrigerator. Bon appétit!

134. Chocolate and Blackberry Smoothie

Ready in about 5 minutes
Servings 2

Serve this smoothie as a well-balanced breakfast or an energy-boosting afternoon snack. You can skip cocoa powder, if desired, and have a completely new taste.

Per serving: 103 Calories; 5.9g Fat; 11g Carbs; 4.1g Protein; 4.4g Sugars

Ingredients

1 cup blackberries
1 cup water
1 tablespoon chia seeds
1 tablespoon cocoa
1/4 teaspoon ground nutmeg
1 tablespoon peanut butter
Liquid Stevia, to taste

Directions

- Add all ingredients to your blender or a food processor.
- Mix until creamy and uniform.

Storing

Pour your smoothie into two glass containers with airtight lids; make sure to fill the containers to the very top. Seal your containers tightly and store in the refrigerator for up to 24 hours.
To freeze, pour the smoothie into freezer-safe jars. They will maintain the best quality for 3 months. Defrost in your refrigerator.

135. Garlicky Savoy Cabbage

Ready in about 25 minutes
Servings 4

Once you ditch animal products, it opens a whole new perspective on nutrition and dieting. You will soon realize that a plant-based diet is a shortcut to successful weight loss.

Per serving: 118 Calories; 7g Fat; 13.4g Carbs; 2.9g Protein; 7.3g Sugars

Ingredients

2 pounds Savoy cabbage, torn into pieces
2 tablespoons almond oil
1 teaspoon garlic, minced
1/2 teaspoon dried basil
1/2 teaspoon red pepper flakes, crushed
Salt and ground black pepper, to the taste

Directions

- Cook Savoy cabbage in a pot of a lightly salted water approximately 20 minutes over a moderate heat. Drain and reserve.
- Now, heat the oil in a sauté pan over a medium-high heat. Now, cook the garlic until just aromatic.
- Add reserved Savoy cabbage, basil, red pepper, salt and black pepper; stir until everything is heated through.
- Taste and adjust the seasonings. Let cool completely.

Storing

Place Savoy cabbage in airtight containers or Ziploc bags; keep in your refrigerator for 3 to 5 days.
Place Savoy cabbage in freezable containers; they can be frozen for up to 10 months. Defrost in the refrigerator or microwave. Bon appétit!

136. Autumn Oven-Roasted Vegetables

Ready in about 45 minutes
Servings 4

If you are looking for just the right recipe for sensational roasted veggies, look no further. Don't forget to slice your veggies into similarly sized pieces and drizzle them generously with olive oil. So good, right?

Per serving: 165 Calories; 14.3g Fat; 10.2g Carbs; 2.1g Protein; 3.7g Sugars

Ingredients

1 red bell pepper, deveined and sliced
1 green bell pepper, deveined and sliced
1 orange bell pepper, deveined and sliced
1/2 head of cauliflower, broken into large florets
2 zucchinis, cut into thick slices
2 medium-sized leeks, quartered
4 garlic cloves, halved
2 thyme sprigs, chopped
1 teaspoon dried sage, crushed
4 tablespoons olive oil
4 tablespoons tomato puree
1 teaspoon mixed whole peppercorns
Sea salt and cayenne pepper, to taste

Directions

- Preheat your oven to 425 degrees F. Sprits a rimmed baking sheet with a nonstick cooking spray.
- Toss all of the above vegetables with seasonings, oil and apple cider vinegar.
- Roast about 40 minutes. Flip vegetables halfway through cook time. Let cool completely.

Storing

Place your vegetables in airtight containers or Ziploc bags; keep in your refrigerator for 3 to 5 days.
Place your vegetables in freezable containers; it will maintain the best quality for 10 months. Defrost in the refrigerator or microwave. Bon appétit!

137. Chocolate and Butternut Squash Smoothie

Ready in about 5 minutes
Servings 2

This luscious, creamy smoothie is worth making! It looks like the perfect snack to bridge the gap between two meals.

Per serving: 71 Calories; 2.3g Fat; 9.1g Carbs; 4.3g Protein; 5g Sugars

Ingredients

2 ½ cups almond milk
1/2 cup baby spinach
2 tablespoons cocoa powder
1/2 cup butternut squash, roasted
1/2 teaspoon ground cinnamon
A pinch of grated nutmeg
A pinch of salt

Directions

- Mix all ingredients in a blender or a food processor.

Storing

Pour your smoothie into two glass containers with airtight lids; make sure to fill the containers to the very top. Seal your containers tightly and store in the refrigerator for up to 24 hours.
To freeze, pour the smoothie into freezer-safe jars. They will maintain the best quality for 3 months. Defrost in your refrigerator.

138. Melt-in-Your-Mouth Hazelnut Chocolate

Ready in about 25 minutes
Servings 8

An easy keto hazelnut chocolate recipe made from pungent cacao butter, Swerve, and roasted hazelnuts. It is kid-friendly and perfect for your keto diet.

Per serving: 140 Calories; 14g Fat; 8.1g Carbs; 2g Protein; 4.2g Sugars

Ingredients

4 ounces cacao butter
1 tablespoon extra-virgin coconut oil
8 tablespoons cocoa powder
1/4 cup Swerve
1/4 teaspoon hazelnut extract
1 teaspoon pure vanilla extract
1/8 teaspoon coarse salt
1/4 teaspoon grated nutmeg
1/2 cup roasted hazelnuts, chopped

Directions

- Melt the cacao butter and coconut oil in a microwave for 1 minute or so.
- Now, stir in cocoa powder, Swerve, hazelnut extract, vanilla extract, salt and nutmeg.
- Pour the mixture into an ice cube mold. Add the roasted hazelnuts and place in your freezer for 20 minutes or until solid.

Storing

Place the homemade chocolate in airtight containers or Ziploc bags; keep in your refrigerator for 7 days.
Place the homemade chocolate in freezable containers; it will maintain the best quality for 4 to 6 months.
Defrost in the refrigerator. Bon appétit!

139. Silky Peanut and Coconut Bark

Ready in about 10 minutes + chilling time
Servings 12

Everyone loves a bark! If you prefer slightly salty bark, add a pinch of crushed Maldon sea salt to the mixture.

Per serving: 316 Calories; 31.6g Fat; 4.6g Carbs; 6.6g Protein; 1.3g Sugars

Ingredients

3/4 cup peanut butter
3/4 cup coconut oil
1 cup Swerve
1 teaspoon pure vanilla extract
1/2 teaspoon pure almond extract
1/2 cup coconut flakes

Directions

- Combine all ingredients in a pan over a moderate heat; cook, stirring continuously, for 4 to 5 minutes.
- Spoon the mixture into a parchment-lined baking sheet. Refrigerate overnight and break your bark into pieces.

Storing

Place your bark in airtight containers or Ziploc bags; keep in your refrigerator for 1 month.
Place your bark in freezable containers; it will maintain the best quality for 4 months. Defrost in the refrigerator. Bon appétit!

140. Raspberry and Peanut Butter Smoothie

Ready in about 5 minutes
Servings 1

Smoothies are one of the best grab-n-go foods of all time! You can use fresh or frozen strawberries and even 1/2 medium-sized peach in this recipe.

Per serving: 114 Calories; 8.2g Fat; 7.9g Carbs; 4.2g Protein; 3.1g Sugars

Ingredients

1/3 cup raspberries
1/2 cup baby spinach leaves
3/4 cup almond milk, unsweetened
1 tablespoon peanut butter
1 teaspoon Swerve

Directions

- Place all ingredients in your blender and puree until creamy, uniform and smooth.

Storing

Pour your smoothie into a glass container with airtight lids; make sure to fill the container to the very top. Seal your container tightly and store in the refrigerator for up to 24 hours.
To freeze, pour the smoothie into a freezer-safe jar. They will maintain the best quality for 3 months. Defrost in your refrigerator.

FAST SNACKS & APPETIZERS

141. Caramelized Garlic Mushrooms

Ready in about 10 minutes
Servings 4

These caramelized mushrooms bring the flavors of summer days to your kitchen. Serve with sour cream and mayo for a full keto experience!

Per serving: 75 Calories; 5.2g Fat; 3.3g Carbs; 2.9g Protein; 0.1g Sugars

Ingredients

2 teaspoons olive oil
1 tablespoon butter
2 cloves garlic, minced
1 pound Portobello mushrooms, sliced
1 tablespoon soy sauce
Salt and pepper, to taste

Directions

- Heat the oil and butter in a large skillet that is preheated over a moderate heat. Add garlic and cook until aromatic, 30 seconds or so.
- Stir in the mushrooms and cook them for 3 minutes, allowing them to caramelize.
- Now, add soy sauce, salt and pepper; cook for 4 minutes more or to desired doneness. Let cool completely.

Storing

Place caramelized mushrooms in airtight containers; keep in your refrigerator for 3 to 5 days.
Place caramelized mushrooms on the parchment-lined baking sheet, about 1-inch apart from each other; freeze for about 2 to 3 hours.
Remove frozen mushrooms to a freezer bag for long-term storage; they will maintain the best quality for 10 to 12 months. Enjoy!

142. Cocktail Meatballs with Romano Cheese

Ready in about 40 minutes
Servings 5

These meatballs are so amazing on their own, you won't need to serve them with anything else. Toothpicks and napkins would be just fine.

Per serving: 244 Calories; 13.3g Fat; 3.7g Carbs; 28.1g Protein; 1.2g Sugars

Ingredients

1/3 pound ground turkey
1/3 pound ground pork
1/3 pound ground beef
2 ounces Romano cheese, grated
2 tablespoons buttermilk
2 eggs, whisked
1/2 yellow onion, chopped
2 cloves garlic, minced
1 tablespoon Dijon mustard
1 teaspoon ancho chili powder
Salt and ground black pepper, to taste
1/2 cup ground almonds

Directions

- Thoroughly combine all of the above ingredients, except for ground almonds, in a mixing dish.
- Grease your hands with oil and roll the mixture into 20 meatballs. Place ground almond in a shallow bowl.
- Toss your meatballs in ground almond until they're completely coated.
- Heat up a nonstick skillet over a moderately high heat. Now, spritz the bottom and sides of the skillet with a nonstick cooking spray.
- Cook your meatballs about 13 minutes, until they're golden brown all around. Let cool completely.

Storing

Place the meatballs in airtight containers or Ziploc bags; keep in your refrigerator for up to 3 to 4 days.
Freeze the meatballs in airtight containers or heavy-duty freezer bags. Freeze up to 3 to 4 months.
To defrost, slowly reheat in a saucepan. Bon appétit!

143. Spicy Tuna Deviled Eggs

Ready in about 20 minutes
Servings 6

Can you imagine a cocktail party without charming deviled eggs? They are mouth-watering, appetizing and so easy to make.

Per serving: 203 Calories; 13.3g Fat; 3.8g Carbs; 17.2g Protein; 1.5g Sugars

Ingredients

12 eggs
1/3 cup mayonnaise
1 can tuna in spring water, drained
1/2 teaspoon smoked cayenne pepper
1/4 teaspoon fresh or dried dill weed
2 pickled jalapenos, minced
Salt and black pepper, to taste

Directions

- Place the eggs in a wide pot; cover with cold water by 1 inch. Bring to a rapid boil.
- Decrease the heat to medium-low; let them simmer an additional 10 minutes.
- Peel the eggs and rinse them under running water.
- Slice each egg in half lengthwise and remove the yolks. Thoroughly combine the yolks with the remaining ingredients.
- Divide the mixture among egg whites.

Storing

Place deviled eggs in an airtight container or Ziploc bag; transfer to your refrigerator; they should be consumed within 2 days.
For freezing, spoon out the yolk mixture from the deviled eggs. Add the egg yolk mixture to an airtight container or Ziploc bag.
Place the container in the freezer for up to 3 months. To defrost, let them sit overnight in the refrigerator until they are fully thawed out.

144. Paprika and Mustard Bacon Chips

Ready in about 20 minutes
Servings 4

You won't miss potato chips, not at all, trust us! Serve with salsa, guacamole or barbecue dip.

Per serving: 118 Calories; 10g Fat; 1.9g Carbs; 5g Protein; 0.4g Sugars

Ingredients

12 bacon strips, cut into small squares
1 tablespoon smoked paprika
1 tablespoon mustard

Directions

- Preheat your oven to 360 degrees F
- Toss the bacon strips with paprika and mustard.
- Arrange bacon squares on a parchment lined baking sheet. Bake for 10 to 15 minutes. Let cool completely.

Storing

Place bacon chips in an airtight container or wrap tightly with heavy-duty aluminum foil; transfer to your refrigerator; they should be consumed within 3 to 4 days.
To freeze, place bacon chips in an airtight container and freeze up to 2 to 3 months. It has been thawed in the refrigerator and can be kept for an additional 3 to 4 days in the refrigerator before serving.
Reheat in your oven until crisp. Enjoy!

145. Easy Rutabaga Fries

Ready in about 35 minutes
Servings 4

Make this grab-and-go quick snack and delight your family especially kids! It's good to know that you can make fries out of almost any type of veggies.

Per serving: 134 Calories; 10.8g Fat; 9.9g Carbs; 1.5g Protein; 6.8g Sugars

Ingredients

1 ½ pounds rutabaga, cut into sticks 1/4-inch wide
3 tablespoons olive oil
Salt and ground black pepper, to taste
1/2 teaspoon cayenne pepper
1/2 teaspoon mustard seeds

Directions

- Add rutabaga sticks to a mixing dish. In another small-sized mixing dish, whisk the other ingredients.
- Add the oil mixture to the rutabaga sticks and toss to coat well.
- Preheat your oven to 440 degrees F. Line a baking sheet with parchment paper.
- Place seasoned rutabaga sticks on the baking sheet. Roast them approximately 30 minutes, turning baking sheet occasionally.
- Transfer the rutabaga fries to the ice water immediately; cool completely.

Storing

Place the rutabaga fries in airtight containers or Ziploc bags; keep in your refrigerator for up to 3 to 5 days.
Arrange the rutabaga fries on a baking sheet in a single layer; freeze for about 2 hours. Transfer frozen rutabaga fries to freezer storage bags. Freeze for up to 12 months.

146. Cauliflower Balls with Greek Yoghurt Sauce

Ready in about 30 minutes
Servings 6

These cauliflower balls can truly be a life-saver on the ketogenic diet! They're shockingly tasty and go wonderfully with a tangy Greek yogurt sauce.

Per serving: 182 Calories; 13.1g Fat; 5.9g Carbs; 11.5g Protein; 2.2g Sugars

Ingredients

1 head cauliflower
1/2 cup Parmesan cheese, grated
3 eggs
1 cup Asiago cheese, shredded
1 onion, finely chopped
1 garlic clove, minced
Salt and black pepper, to taste

For Greek Yoghurt Sauce:
1 cup Greek yogurt
1 teaspoon lemon juice
1 garlic clove, minced
1 tablespoon mayonnaise
1 tablespoon olive oil
1/2 teaspoon dried dill weed

Directions

- Cook the cauliflower in a large pot of salted water until tender, about 6 minutes; cut into florets.
- Preheat your oven to 400 degrees F. Coat a baking pan with parchment paper.
- Mash the cauliflower with Parmesan, eggs, cheese, onion, garlic, salt and black pepper; shape the mixture into balls.
- Bake for 22 minutes or until they are slightly crisp.
- To make the sauce, whisk all remaining ingredients. Let cool completely.

Storing

Transfer the balls to the airtight containers and place in your refrigerator for up to 3 to 4 days.
For freezing, place the balls in freezer safe containers and freeze up to 1 month. Defrost in the microwave for a few minutes.
Place the sauce in a glass jar with an airtight lid; keep in your refrigerator for up to 3 days

147. Dippable Cheese Crisps

Ready in about 20 minutes
Servings 6

Healthy, low-carb and guilt-free, these spicy crisps might become your favorite snack for movie night at home.

Per serving: 225 Calories; 19.3g Fat; 0.6g Carbs; 12.1g Protein; 0.3g Sugars

Ingredients

1 cup Romano cheese, finely shredded
1 cup Pepper Jack cheese, shredded
4 slices bacon, cooked and crumbled
1 jalapeño, finely chopped
1/4 teaspoon red pepper flakes
1/2 teaspoon ground cumin
1/4 teaspoon cardamom
Salt and pepper, to taste

Directions

- Begin by preheating your oven to 400 degrees F. Line a baking sheet with a sheet of parchment paper.
- Spoon 1 tablespoon of Romano cheese into a small mound on the parchment paper. Top with about 1 tablespoon of shredded Pepper Jack cheese.
- Add bacon and chopped jalapeño. Sprinkle with red pepper, cumin, cardamom, salt, and pepper; gently flatten each mound.
- Bake approximately 12 minutes. Transfer the baking sheet to a wire rack to cool completely.

Storing

Divide crisps between two airtight containers or Ziploc bags; keep in your refrigerator for up to 4 days. To freeze, divide crisps between two airtight containers. Freeze up to 2 months. Defrost and reheat in your oven until it is crisp. Enjoy!

148. Crock Pot Little Smokies

Ready in about 2 hours 30 minutes
Servings 6

When you're looking for just the right thing to serve for an easy and effective appetizer, this recipe will fit the bill. You can come up with your favorite combination of aromatics.

Per serving: 271 Calories; 22.2g Fat; 4.5g Carbs; 12.3g Protein; 0.6g Sugars

Ingredients

1 ½ pounds cocktail franks
3 tablespoons wholegrain mustard
1 bottle barbecue sauce
1 tablespoon Swerve
1 teaspoon onion powder

Directions

- Heat up a pan over a moderately high heat; now, brown the sausage about 3 minutes.
- Treat your crockpot with a nonstick cooking spray. Add all of the above ingredients and stir well.
- Cook on Low heat setting for 2 ½ hours. Let cool completely.

Storing

Transfer the little smokies to the airtight containers and place in your refrigerator for up to 3 to 4 days. For freezing, place the little smokies in freezer safe containers or wrap tightly with heavy-duty aluminum foil; freeze up to 1 to 2 months. Defrost in the microwave for a few minutes. Enjoy!

149. Muffin Appetizer with Herbes de Provence

Ready in about 20 minutes
Servings 6

Are you craving the flavors of Southern France? Herbes de Provence is a spice that features rosemary, marjoram, thyme and savory as main ingredients. This mix may include citrus zest, fennel seeds, and tarragon too.

Per serving: 269 Calories; 20.7g Fat; 7g Carbs; 15.5g Protein; 1.3g Sugars

Ingredients

Nonstick cooking spray
1/3 cup flaxseed meal
2/3 cup almond flour
2 tablespoons xylitol
2 teaspoons psyllium
1/8 teaspoon kosher salt
1/8 teaspoon grated nutmeg
1 teaspoon herbes de Provence
1/2 teaspoon baking powder
2 eggs
1/2 cup yogurt
10 slices salami, chopped

Directions

- Start by preheating your oven to 360 degrees F. Lightly grease a muffin pan with a nonstick cooking spray.
- Thoroughly combine flaxseed meal with almond flour, xylitol, psyllium, salt, nutmeg, herbes de Provence and baking powder; stir until well combined.
- Now, stir in the eggs, yogurt, and salami. Press the mixture into prepared muffin cups.
- Bake about 15 minutes and transfer to a wire rack to cool slightly before removing from the muffin pan. Let cool completely.

Storing

Divide muffins between two airtight containers; keep in the refrigerator for a week.
For freezing, divide the muffins among three Ziploc bags and freeze up to 3 months. Defrost in your microwave for a couple of minutes. Enjoy!

150. Pepperoni and Cheese Bites

Ready in about 10 minutes
Servings 5

This is another keto snack recipe, bursting with amazing flavor. You can add any deli cheese such as provolone or mozzarella.

Per serving: 341 Calories; 30.6g Fat; 3.4g Carbs; 12.8g Protein; 0.5g Sugars

Ingredients

5 ounces Pepperoni, chopped
5 ounces cream cheese
4 large egg yolks, hard-boiled
2 tablespoons mayonnaise
1 teaspoon deli mustard
1/2 teaspoon paprika
2 tablespoons hemp hearts

Directions

- Add Pepperoni, cheese and egg yolks to a mixing dish; stir to combine well.
- Now, stir in mayonnaise, mustard, and paprika; stir again.
- Shape the mixture into 10 balls.
- Place hemp hearts on a medium plate; roll each ball through to coat. Arrange these balls on a nice serving platter and serve. Let cool completely.

Storing

Divide these balls between two airtight containers or Ziploc bags; keep in your refrigerator for up 3 to 4 days.
For freezing, place balls in two airtight containers. Freeze up to 1 month. Defrost in the refrigerator. Bon appétit!

151. Chicken Wings with Tomato Dip

Ready in about 50 minutes
Servings 6

This is the classic recipe for chicken wings with a little keto twist. Crispy and flavorful, chicken wings go wonderfully with fresh tomato dip.

Per serving: 236 Calories; 13.5g Fat; 9g Carbs; 19.4g Protein; 6.8g Sugars

Ingredients

12 chicken wings
Salt and pepper, to taste
For the Tomato Dip:
4 ripe tomatoes, crushed
1 onion, finely chopped
1 cup mango, peeled and chopped
1 teaspoon chili pepper, deveined and finely minced
2 heaping tablespoons cilantro, finely chopped
2 tablespoons lime juice

Directions

- Start by preheating your oven to 400 degrees F. Set a wire rack inside a rimmed baking sheet.
- Season chicken wings with salt and pepper. Bake wings approximately 45 minutes or until skin is crispy.
- Then, thoroughly combine all ingredients for the tomato dip. Let cool completely.

Storing

Place chicken wings in airtight containers or Ziploc bags; keep in your refrigerator for up 3 to 4 days.
For freezing, place chicken wings in airtight containers or heavy-duty freezer bags. Freeze up to 3 months. Once thawed in the refrigerator, heat in the preheated oven at 375 degrees F for 20 to 25 minutes or until heated through.
Place the tomato dip in a glass jar with an airtight lid; keep in your refrigerator for 3 to 4 days. Enjoy!

152. Dilled Chicken Wingettes with Goat Cheese Dip

Ready in about 1 hour 15 minutes
Servings 10

Here's an ultimate comfort food perfect for any occasion, from a cocktail party and Super Bowl party to kid's birthday parties!

Per serving: 227 Calories; 10.2g Fat; 0.4g Carbs; 31.5g Protein; 0.2g Sugars

Ingredients

Nonstick cooking spray
3 pounds chicken wingettes
Salt and black pepper, to taste
1/4 teaspoon smoked paprika
1 teaspoon dried dill weed

For Goat Cheese Dip:
1 cup goat cheese, crumbled
1/3 cup mayonnaise
2 tablespoons Greek-style yogurt
1 teaspoon Dijon mustard
2 cloves garlic, smashed
1 teaspoon onion powder
1/2 teaspoon ground cumin
1/4 cup fresh coriander leaves, finely chopped

Directions

- Preheat your oven to 390 degrees F. Set a wire rack inside a rimmed baking sheet. Spritz the rack with a nonstick cooking oil.
- Toss chicken wingettes with salt, pepper, paprika, and dill.
- Place the chicken wingettes skin side up on the rack. Bake in the lower quarter of the oven for 30 to 35 minutes.
- Turn the oven up to 420 degrees F. Bake for a further 40 minutes on the higher shelf, rotating the baking sheet once.
- In the meantime, combine goat cheese, mayo, yogurt, mustard, garlic, onion powder, ground cumin, and coriander. Let cool completely.

Storing

Place wingettes in airtight containers or Ziploc bags; keep in your refrigerator for up 3 to 4 days.
For freezing, place wingettes in airtight containers or heavy-duty freezer bags. Freeze up to 3 months. Once thawed in the refrigerator, heat in the preheated oven at 375 degrees F for 20 to 25 minutes or until heated through.
Place the sauce in a glass jar with an airtight lid; keep in your refrigerator for up 3 to 4 days. Enjoy!

153. Celery Root French Fries with Pine Nuts

Ready in about 35 minutes
Servings 6

Here's an amazing low-carb alternative to potato fries. Even if you don't follow a ketogenic diet, you will surely enjoy roasted vegetable sticks.

Per serving: 96 Calories; 8.5g Fat; 4.1g Carbs; 1.5g Protein; 1.7g Sugars

Ingredients

1 ½ pounds celery root, cut into sticks
Salt and ground black pepper, to taste
1/2 teaspoon cayenne pepper
2 tablespoons olive oil
1 tablespoon Cajun seasoning
1/4 cup pine nuts, coarsely ground

Directions

- Preheat your oven to 390 degrees F. Line a baking sheet with a parchment paper or Silpat mat.
- Mix celery root, salt, black pepper, cayenne pepper, olive oil and Cajun seasoning in a mixing dish.
- Arrange celery sticks on the prepared baking sheet and bake for 30 minutes, flipping every 10 minutes to promote even cooking; sprinkle with pine nuts. Let cool completely.

Storing

Place your fries in airtight containers or Ziploc bags; keep in your refrigerator for up to 3 to 5 days.
To freeze, arrange your fries on a baking sheet in a single layer; freeze for about 2 hours. Transfer the frozen fries to freezer storage bags. Freeze for up to 12 months. Bon appétit!

154. Cheese-Stuffed Cocktail Meatballs

Ready in about 25 minutes
Servings 10

Here is a keto twist on an old party favorite! Monterey Jack cheese tucked inside each meatball creates a burst of flavor.

Per serving: 186 Calories; 9.6g Fat; 1.2g Carbs; 23.9g Protein; 0.4g Sugars

Ingredients

1/2 pound ground turkey
1 pound ground pork
1/3 cup Parmesan cheese, freshly grated
Sea salt and ground black pepper, to taste
1 teaspoon red pepper flakes, crushed
1 teaspoon oyster sauce
1/2 cup onion, finely chopped
2 cloves garlic, minced
2 eggs
1 cup Monterey Jack cheese, cubed

Directions

- Start by preheating your oven to 390 degrees F. Coat a baking pan with parchment paper.
- Thoroughly combine all ingredients, except for Monterey Jack cheese, in a mixing bowl.
- Shape this meat mixture into 40 meatballs. Press 1 cheese cube into the middle of each meatball; be sure to seal it inside.
- Gently place the meatballs on the prepared baking pan.
- Bake about 20 minutes until they are browned and slightly crisp on top. Let cool completely.

Storing

Place the meatballs in airtight containers or Ziploc bags; keep in your refrigerator for up to 3 to 4 days.
Freeze the meatballs in airtight containers or heavy-duty freezer bags. Freeze up to 3 to 4 months.
To defrost, slowly reheat in a saucepan. Bon appétit!

155. Sriracha and Parm Chicken Wings

Ready in about 1 hour 10 minutes
Servings 6

The next-level wings your guests will love! These wings carry some of the flavors of Mexican cuisine, so you can increase or reduce the spiciness by controlling the amount of Sriracha chili sauce.

Per serving: 312 Calories; 23g Fat; 0.9g Carbs; 24.6g Protein; 0.1g Sugars

Ingredients

2 pounds chicken wings
Coarse salt and freshly ground black pepper, to taste
1/2 teaspoon smoked cayenne pepper
1 tablespoon balsamic vinegar
2 teaspoons Sriracha chili sauce
2 cloves garlic, smashed
1 stick butter
1 cup Parmesan cheese
2 tablespoons oyster sauce
1/2 cup fresh chives, chopped

Directions

- Preheat an oven to 420 degrees F. Set a metal rack on top of a baking sheet.
- Season chicken wings with salt, black pepper, cayenne pepper. Now, roast the wings until the skin is crisp, about 45 minutes.
- In the meantime, simmer the vinegar, Sriracha, and garlic until the mixture has reduced slightly, about 12 minutes.
- In a shallow bowl, combine softened butter with parmesan cheese and oyster sauce.
- Next, toss chicken wings with Sriracha mixture. After that, dredge chicken wings in parmesan mixture until fully coated; then place on the baking sheet.
- Bake an additional 10 minutes; add fresh chopped chives. Let cool completely.

Storing

Place chicken wings in airtight containers or Ziploc bags; keep in your refrigerator for up 3 to 4 days.
For freezing, place chicken wings in airtight containers or heavy-duty freezer bags. Freeze up to 3 months. Once thawed in the refrigerator, heat in the preheated oven at 375 degrees F for 20 to 25 minutes or until heated through. Enjoy!

156. Mediterranean Cheese Ball

Ready in about 10 minutes
Servings 6

This is the cheese ball you can serve at any party. Like mini cheese balls but way more fun!

Per serving: 182 Calories; 15.5g Fat; 3g Carbs; 7.6g Protein; 1.2g Sugars

Ingredients

6 ounces Neufchatel cheese
1/4 cup aioli
1 tablespoon tomato paste
6 slices of Iberian ham, chopped
6 Kalamata olives, pitted and chopped
1 teaspoon dried basil
1 teaspoon dried oregano
1 teaspoon dried rosemary

Directions

- Thoroughly combine Neufchatel cheese, aioli, tomato paste, chopped ham and olives in a mixing bowl; mix until everything is homogeneous.
- In a shallow dish, combine dried basil, oregano, and rosemary.
- Shape the mixture into a ball. Roll the ball in the herb mixture.

Storing

Wrap the cheese ball tightly in a plastic wrap. Now, wrap it in aluminum foil; shape with your hands.
Keep in your refrigerator for up 3 to 4 days.
For freezing, wrap tightly in a resealable freezer bag. Freeze up to 2 months. To defrost, remove from freezer the morning before you want to serve.

157. Easy and Spicy Shrimp Appetizer

Ready in about 15 minutes
Servings 6

Shrimp is a real crowd pleaser. Toss with whatever spices you have on hand and sear quickly in the preheated pan. Serve with a classic Marinara sauce.

Per serving: 107 Calories; 4.9g Fat; 1g Carbs; 15.3g Protein; 0.2g Sugars

Ingredients

2 tablespoons coconut oil, room temperature
1 pound shrimp, deveined and shelled, tail on
1 teaspoon garlic, minced
1/2 cup scallions, chopped
1 teaspoon ancho chili powder
2 tablespoons apple cider vinegar
1/4 cup chicken stock
1 teaspoon paprika
Salt and ground black pepper, to taste

Directions

- Heat coconut oil in a frying pan over a moderately high flame. Now, cook shrimp together with garlic and scallions.
- Add chili powder, vinegar, and chicken stock and continue to cook 3 minutes more. Season with paprika, salt, and pepper to taste. Let cool completely.

Storing

Place shrimp in airtight containers or Ziploc bags; keep in your refrigerator for up 3 to 4 days.
For freezing, arrange cooked shrimp in a single layer on a baking tray; place in the freezer for about 15 minutes, or until it begins to harden.
Transfer frozen shrimp to heavy-duty freezer bags. Freeze up to 3 months. Defrost in your refrigerator. Enjoy!

158. Saucy Cheesy Baby Carrots

Ready in about 35 minutes
Servings 6

Here is a keto snack worth trying for the next dinner party! A great way to eat baby carrots!

Per serving: 216 Calories; 18.7g Fat; 9.4g Carbs; 3.5g Protein; 5.4g Sugars

Ingredients

1 ½ pounds baby carrots, florets separated
1 stick butter, melted
1/2 teaspoon coarse salt
1/4 teaspoon ground black pepper
1/4 teaspoon ground cumin
1/4 teaspoon dried dill weed
1/2 cup Asiago cheese, grated

Directions

- Begin by preheating your oven to 400 degrees F.
- Coat baby carrots with melted butter, salt, pepper, cumin and dill weed.
- Bake for 30 minutes in the middle of the preheated oven, stirring once or twice.
- Top with shredded Asiago cheese and bake an additional 5 minutes or until cheese is slightly browned. Let cool completely.

Storing

Place baby carrots in airtight containers or Ziploc bags; keep in your refrigerator for up to 3 to 5 days. To freeze, arrange baby carrots on a baking sheet in a single layer; freeze for about 2 hours. Transfer to freezer storage bags. Freeze for up to 3 months. Bon appétit!

159. Oven-Baked Zucchini Bites

Ready in about 40 minutes
Servings 4

A buttery-like texture of zucchini and its mild flavor, when prepared in this manner, pair so well with seasonings and egg whites.

Per serving: 91 Calories; 6.1g Fat; 6g Carbs; 4.2g Protein; 3.5g Sugars

Ingredients

4 zucchinis, cut into thick slices
2 tablespoons butter, melted
2 egg whites
Coarse salt and crushed black peppercorns, to taste
1/2 teaspoon red pepper flakes, crushed
1/2 teaspoon dried dill weed

Directions

- Begin by preheating an oven to 420 degrees F. Coat a rimmed baking sheet with parchment paper or Silpat mat.
- In a mixing bowl, whisk the butter with two egg whites. Add the seasonings.
- Now, toss the zucchini slices with this mixture.
- Arrange coated zucchini slices on the baking sheet; bake for 35 minutes until the slices are golden, turning once.
- Check for doneness and bake another 5 minutes if needed. Let cool completely.

Storing

Place zucchini in airtight containers or Ziploc bags; keep in your refrigerator for 3 to 5 days.
Place zucchini in a freezable container; they can be frozen for up to 10 to 12 months. Bake the thawed zucchini at 200 degrees F until they are completely warm. Enjoy!

160. Gruyère Cheese and Kale Muffins

Ready in about 25 minutes
Servings 6

It's going to be the best muffins ever! Try them and enjoy their wonderful taste!

Per serving: 275 Calories; 15.8g Fat; 7.2g Carbs; 21.6g Protein; 1.4g Sugars

Ingredients

5 eggs
1/2 cup full-fat milk
Sea salt, to taste
1/2 teaspoon dried basil
1 ½ cups Gruyère cheese, grated
10 ounces kale, cooked and drained
1/2 pound prosciutto, chopped

Directions

- Start by preheating your oven to 360 degrees F. Spritz a muffin tin with a cooking spray.
- Whisk the milk, salt, basil and cheese in a mixing bowl. Toss in kale and prosciutto. Spoon the batter into each muffin cup (3/4 full).
- Bake for 20 to 25 minutes. Let cool completely.

Storing

Wrap the muffins tightly with heavy-duty aluminum foil or plastic wrap. Then, keep in your refrigerator for up to 3 to 4 days.
For freezing, wrap the muffins tightly to prevent freezer burn. Freeze up to 3 to 4 months. Defrost in the refrigerator. Bon appétit!

VEGETARIAN

161. Roasted Turnips and Bell Peppers

Ready in about 35 minutes
Servings 6

Turnip is loaded with vitamins B1, B3, B5, B6, A, C, E, and K as well as minerals such as potassium, iron, manganese, copper, and calcium. It contains omega-3 fatty acids too.

Per serving: 137 Calories; 11.1g Fat; 9.1g Carbs; 1.2g Protein; 5g Sugars

Ingredients

1 ½ pounds turnips, cut into wedges
1 bell pepper, sliced
1 fresh jalapeño, minced
3 tablespoons ghee, cubed
1 teaspoon dried marjoram
1 onion, thinly sliced
1 garlic clove, minced
2 tablespoons olive oil
1 teaspoon salt
1/2 teaspoon freshly ground black pepper
1/2 teaspoon cayenne pepper

Directions

- Begin by preheating an oven to 425 degrees F. Lightly grease a baking dish with a nonstick cooking spray.
- Toss the turnips and bell peppers with the remaining ingredients.
- Roast the turnips and peppers for 25 to 35 or until they're softened. Taste and adjust the seasonings. Let cool completely.

Storing

Transfer the vegetables to the airtight containers and place in your refrigerator for up to 3 to 5 days.
For freezing, place the vegetables in freezer safe containers and freeze up to 8 to 10 months. Defrost in the microwave for a few minutes. Bon appétit!

162. Cheesy Broccoli Casserole

Ready in about 25 minutes
Servings 3

What are you up to this mooring? This ketogenic breakfast is both, light and fulfilling.

Per serving: 195 Calories; 12.7g Fat; 10.7g Carbs; 11.6g Protein; 2g Sugars

Ingredients

3 tablespoons avocado oil
1 shallot, minced
1/2 teaspoon garlic, minced
1 head broccoli, cut into small florets
3 eggs, well-beaten
1/2 cup half-and-half
1/2 teaspoon dried basil
1/2 teaspoon turmeric powder
Kosher salt and cayenne pepper, to taste
2 ounces Monterey Jack cheese, shredded

Directions

- Preheat your oven to 310 degrees F.
- Melt avocado oil in a pan over a moderate heat. Now, sauté the shallots and garlic for a few minutes. Stir in the broccoli florets and cook until they're tender. Transfer the mixture to a lightly greased casserole dish.
- In a separate mixing bowl, combine the eggs with half-and-half, basil, turmeric, salt and cayenne pepper.
- Pour the egg mixture over the broccoli mixture. Bake for 20 minutes or until set. Check the temperature with an instant-read food thermometer. Add Monterey Jack cheese. Let cool completely.

Storing

Slice the casserole into three pieces. Divide the pieces between three airtight containers; it will last for 3 to 4 days in the refrigerator.
For freezing, place each portion in a separate heavy-duty freezer bag. Freeze up to 2 to 3 months. Defrost in the microwave or refrigerator. Bon appétit!

163. Family Vegetable Bake

Ready in about 1 hour
Servings 4

Here's one of the easiest keto casseroles to make for an easy, no-stress family dinner. We opted for Taco seasoning but you can toss in whatever spices and herbs you have on hand!

Per serving: 159 Calories; 10.4g Fat; 12.7g Carbs; 6.4g Protein; 5.1g Sugars

Ingredients

1 large eggplant, cut into thick slices
1 tomato, diced
1/2 garlic head, crushed
1 medium-sized leek, sliced
1 celery, peeled and diced
1 Habanero pepper, minced
1 teaspoon Taco seasoning mix
2 tablespoons extra-virgin olive oil
1 tablespoon fresh sage leaves, chopped
1/3 cup Parmigiano-Reggiano cheese, shredded

Directions

- Place the eggplant in a medium-sized bowl; sprinkle with salt and let it stand for 30 minutes; now, drain and rinse the eggplant slices.
- Meanwhile, preheat your oven to 345 degrees F. Spritz a casserole dish with a nonstick cooking spray.
- Mix the vegetables along with seasoning, olive oil, and sage in the prepared casserole dish.
- Roast the vegetables approximately 20 minutes. Scatter shredded cheese over the top and bake an additional 10 minutes. Let cool completely.

Storing

Cut this casserole into four pieces. Place each piece in a separate airtight container or Ziploc bag; keep for 3 to 4 days in the refrigerator.
To freeze, place each piece in a separate heavy-duty freezer bag. Freeze up to 2 to 3 months. Defrost in the microwave or refrigerator. Bon appétit!

164. Vegetables à la Grecque

Ready in about 15 minutes
Servings 4

This authentic Greek sauté can be adapted according to what is in season. Feel free to top these amazing vegetables with Greek cheese like Halloumi.

Per serving: 318 Calories; 24.3g Fat; 9.1g Carbs; 15.4g Protein; 5.7g Sugars

Ingredients

2 tablespoons olive oil
2 garlic cloves, minced
1/2 cup red onion, chopped
1/2 pound button mushrooms, chopped
1 cup cauliflower, cut into small florets
1 medium-sized eggplant, chopped
1 teaspoon dried basil
1 teaspoon dried oregano
1 rosemary sprig, leaves picked
1 thyme sprig, leaves picked
1/2 cup tomato sauce
1/4 cup dry white wine
8 ounces Halloumi cheese, cubed

Directions

- Heat olive oil in a saucepan over a moderately high heat. Now, sauté, garlic for 1 to 1½ minutes.
- Now, stir in the onion, mushrooms, cauliflower, and eggplant; cook an additional 5 minutes, stirring periodically.
- Add the seasonings, tomato sauce, and wine; continue to cook for 4 more minutes. Remove from heat and top with Halloumi cheese. Let cool completely.

Storing

Divide the vegetables into four portions; divide the portions between four airtight containers; keep in your refrigerator for up 3 to 5 days.
For freezing, wrap them tightly with plastic wrap and place in airtight containers. Freeze up to 10 to 12 months. Defrost in the refrigerator. Bon appétit!

165. Roasted Asparagus with Feta Cheese

Ready in about 15 minutes
Servings 6

Asparagus and soft white cheese combine very well! Serve as a side dish or a complete vegetarian meal.

Per serving: 128 Calories; 9.4g Fat; 6.5g Carbs; 6.4g Protein; 3.3g Sugars

Ingredients

1 ½ pounds asparagus spears
2 tablespoons butter, melted
2 green onions, chopped
2 garlic cloves, minced
Salt and black pepper, to the taste
1 cup feta cheese, crumbled
1/2 cup fresh parsley, roughly chopped

Directions

- Preheat an oven to 420 degrees F.
- Drizzle the asparagus with the melted butter. Toss with green onions, garlic, salt, and black pepper.
- Place the asparagus on a lightly-greased baking pan in a single layer. Roast for about 14 minutes.
- Scatter crumbled feta over the warm asparagus spears. Garnish with fresh parsley. Let cool completely.

Storing

Place the mixture in airtight containers; keep in your refrigerator for 3 to 5 days.
For freezing, place them in a freezable container; they can be frozen for 10 to 12 months. Enjoy!

166. Spicy Vegetarian Delight

Ready in about 15 minutes
Servings 4

If you prefer a more authentic Mexican flavor, you can make your own enchilade sauce. It is also budget-friendly because you can freeze leftovers for later.

Per serving: 290 Calories; 21.7g Fat; 17.5g Carbs; 10.6g Protein; 3.7g Sugars

Ingredients

2 tablespoons olive oil
2 small-sized shallots, chopped
1 garlic clove, minced
1 pound cremini mushroom, sliced
1/2 teaspoon salt
1/2 teaspoon ground black pepper
1 cup tomatillo, chopped
4 eggs
1/4 cup enchilada sauce
1 medium-sized avocado, pitted and mashed

Directions

- Heat olive oil in a saucepan over a moderate flame. Now, cook the shallot and garlic until just tender and fragrant.
- Now, add the mushrooms and stir until they're tender. Season with salt and pepper; stir in chopped tomatillo.
- Stir in the eggs and scramble them well. Top with enchilada sauce; top with avocado slices. Let cool completely.

Storing

Place the mixture in airtight containers; keep in your refrigerator for 4 days.
For freezing, place them in a freezable container; they can be frozen for 6 months. Enjoy!

167. Bell Pepper Casserole with Appenzeller Cheese

Ready in about 1 hour
Servings 4

Make this healthy and delicious alternative to the traditional casserole recipe. Looks like the perfect family meal!

Per serving: 408 Calories; 28.9g Fat; 13.6g Carbs; 24.9g Protein; 6.5g Sugars

Ingredients

8 bell peppers
3/4 pound Appenzeller cheese, shredded
2 red onions, thinly sliced
1 garlic clove, crushed
6 whole eggs
1/3 cup sour cream
Sea salt and ground black pepper, to taste
1 teaspoon smoked paprika

Directions

- Preheat an oven to 470 degrees F. Arrange the peppers on a baking sheet in a single layer.
- Bake the peppers in the preheated oven until the skins are browned and blackened, about 20 minutes.
- Turn them over and bake another 10 to 15 minutes. Remove your peppers from the oven; cover with a plastic wrap and allow them to steam for 1 hour.
- Then, remove the skins, stems, and seeds. Place 4 peppers in a lightly oiled casserole dish.
- Top with half of the shredded Appenzeller; add a layer of sliced onions and crushed garlic. Place another layer of roasted peppers, followed by the remaining Appenzeller.
- In a mixing dish, whisk the eggs with sour cream, salt, pepper, and paprika. Pour the mixture over the peppers. Cover tightly with a piece of foil and bake about 20 minutes.
- Next, remove the foil and bake another 20 minutes. Let cool completely.

Storing

Cut this casserole into four pieces. Place each piece in a separate airtight container or Ziploc bag; keep for 3 to 4 days in the refrigerator.
To freeze, place each piece in a separate heavy-duty freezer bag. Freeze up to 2 to 3 months. Defrost in the microwave or refrigerator. Bon appétit!

168. Sautéed Spinach with Cottage Cheese

Ready in about 10 minutes
Servings 4

If you are a vegetarian and you are new to the ketogenic diet, you might be wondering what type of foods you could eat. This recipe offers an answer so keep it in your back pocket.

Per serving: 208 Calories; 13.5g Fat; 11g Carbs; 14.5g Protein; 1.2g Sugars

Ingredients

1/2 stick butter
2 garlic cloves, minced
2 pounds spinach leaves, rinsed and torn into pieces
1 teaspoon salt
1/2 teaspoon cayenne pepper
1/4 teaspoon turmeric powder
1 cup cottage cheese

Directions

Melt the butter in a Dutch oven and sauté the garlic until it's just browned.
Add the spinach leaves, salt, cayenne pepper, and turmeric powder; cook another 2 to 3 minutes over a moderate heat, adding a splash of warm water if needed.
Next, turn the heat on high, and cook for 1 to 2 minutes more, stirring often. Taste and adjust the seasonings.
Top with cottage cheese. Let cool completely.

Storing

Place the mixture in airtight containers; keep in your refrigerator for 3 to 5 days.
For freezing, place them in a freezable container; they can be frozen for 4 to 5 months. Enjoy!

169. Family Pizza with Spring Vegetables

Ready in about 25 minutes
Servings 4

This fresh low-carb pizza features the tang of two kinds of cheese as well as the freshness of spring vegetables such as baby lettuce, red and green chard, green oak, frisee, etc.

Per serving: 234 Calories; 16.1g Fat; 11.1g Carbs; 13.6g Protein; 5.5g Sugars

Ingredients

For the Crust:
A spray coating
1 pound cauliflower
1/2 cup Edam cheese
4 medium-sized eggs
1⁄4 cup heavy cream
1 tablespoon basil-infused oil
Salt, to taste

For the Topping:
1 cup spring mix
3/4 cup tomato sauce, sugar-free
2 tablespoons chives, finely chopped
1 tablespoon fresh sage
1/4 cup Kalamata olives, pitted and sliced
1 cup mozzarella cheese

Directions

- Cook the cauliflower in a large pot of salted water until it is just tender; cut into florets and add the remaining ingredients for the crust.
- Then, preheat your oven to 380 degrees F; add an oven rack to the middle of the oven. Lightly grease a baking pan with a thin layer of a spray coating.
- Spread the crust mixture onto the bottom of the prepared baking pan. Bake for 15 minutes or until the crust is firm and golden.
- Remove from the oven and add the remaining ingredients, ending with mozzarella cheese; bake until the cheese has completely melted.
- Add a few grinds of black pepper if desired. Let cool completely.

Storing

Cut the pizza into four pieces. Place each of them in an airtight container; place in the refrigerator for up to 3 to 4 days.
To freeze, place in separate Ziploc bags and freeze up to 3 months. Defrost in your microwave for a few minutes. Enjoy!

170. Kohlrabi with Thick Mushroom Sauce

Ready in about 25 minutes
Servings 4

Use a vegetable peeler to peel off the tough outer leaves of the kohlrabi. Its mild flavor pairs perfectly with other vegetables and different sauces.

Per serving: 220 Calories; 20g Fat; 8.3g Carbs; 4g Protein; 3.1g Sugars

Ingredients

3/4 pound kohlrabi, trimmed and thinly sliced
3 tablespoons butter
1/2 pound mushrooms, sliced
1/2 cup scallions, chopped
1 garlic clove, minced
1 teaspoon sea salt
1/2 teaspoon ground black pepper
1/4 teaspoon red pepper flakes
1 ½ cups double cream

Directions

- Parboil kohlrabi in a large pot of salted water for 7 to 9 minutes. Drain and set aside.
- Warm the butter over medium-high heat. Sauté the mushrooms, scallions, and garlic until tender and fragrant.
- Season with salt, black pepper, and red pepper flakes.
- Slowly stir in double cream, whisking continuously until the sauce has thickened, about 8 to 12 minutes.
- Pour the mushroom sauce over the kohlrabi. Let cool completely.

Storing

Transfer the vegetables to the airtight containers and place in your refrigerator for up to 3 to 5 days.
For freezing, place the vegetables in freezer safe containers and freeze up to 8 to 10 months. Defrost in the microwave for a few minutes. Bon appétit!

DESSERTS

171. Melt-in-Your-Mouth Chocolate Squares

Ready in about 25 minutes + chilling time
Servings 10

Slightly sweetened with stevia, these chocolate squares are going to be great for a family dessert or midnight snack. A chocolate explosion in your mouth!

Per serving: 119 Calories; 11.7g Fat; 9.2g Carbs; 1.1g Protein; 0.8g Sugars

Ingredients

1/2 cup coconut flour
1 cup almond flour
2 packets stevia
1/4 teaspoon cardamom
1/2 teaspoon star anise, ground
1/2 teaspoon coconut extract
1 teaspoon pure vanilla extract
1 tablespoon rum
A pinch of table salt
1/2 stick butter, cold
1 ½ cups double cream
8 ounces bittersweet chocolate chips, sugar-free

Directions

- Preheat an oven to 330 degrees F. Now, line a baking dish with parchment paper.
- Add flour, stevia, cardamom, anise, coconut extract, vanilla extract, rum and salt to your food processor. Blitz until everything is well combined.
- Cut in cold butter and process to combine again.
- Press the batter into the bottom of the prepared baking dish. Bake about 13 minutes; transfer to a wire rack to cool slightly.
- To make the filling, bring double cream to a simmer in a pan. Add the chocolate and whisk until uniform. Spread over crust and cut into squares. Let cool completely.

Storing

Wrap the chocolate squares tightly with heavy-duty aluminum foil or plastic wrap. Then, keep in your refrigerator for up to 7 days.
These chocolate squares can be frozen in an airtight container. Put a piece of baking parchment between each square to prevent them from sticking together. Freeze up to 4 months. Defrost in the refrigerator. Bon appétit!

172. Frozen Cocoa and Almond Dessert

Ready in about 10 minutes + chilling time
Servings 6

This easy almond recipe comes together quickly and freezes for a couple of hours. A real feast for everyone who has a sweet tooth!

Per serving: 84 Calories; 8.9g Fat; 1.5g Carbs; 0.8g Protein; 0.2g Sugars

Ingredients

1/2 stick butter, melted
1/2 teaspoon vanilla paste
10 drops liquid stevia
2 tablespoons cocoa powder
2 tablespoons almonds, chopped

Directions

- Melt the butter, vanilla paste, and liquid stevia in a pan that is preheated over a moderate heat.
- Stir in cocoa powder and stir well to combine.
- Spoon the mixture into 12 molds of a silicone candy mold tray. Scatter chopped almonds on top. Freeze until set.

Storing

Place dessert in airtight containers. Keep in your refrigerator for up to 8 days.
Freeze up to 3 to 4 months. Defrost in the refrigerator. Bon appétit!

173. Peanut Ice Cream

Ready in about 10 minutes + chilling time
Servings 4

This is probably only ice cream recipe you'll ever need on a ketogenic diet! This is an extremely versatile recipe because you can experiment with different flavors. Consider adding frozen berries, fresh mint or walnuts.

Per serving: 305 Calories; 18.3g Fat; 4.5g Carbs; 1g Protein; 0.5g Sugars

Ingredients

1 ¼ cups almond milk
1/3 cup whipped cream
17 drops liquid stevia
1/2 cup peanuts, chopped
1/2 teaspoon xanthan gum

Directions

- Combine all of the above ingredients, except for xanthan gum, with an electric mixer.
- Now, stir in xanthan gum, whisking constantly, until the mixture is thick. Then, prepare your ice cream in a machine following manufacturer's instructions.

Storing

Spoon your ice cream in an airtight container. Store your ice cream in the very back of the freezer. Freeze up to 2 to 4 months. Bon appétit!

174. Vanilla Keto Pudding

Ready in about 1 hour
Servings 6

Sometimes you just have a craving for vanilla... This comfort-food recipe is sugar-free and guilt-free!

Per serving: 248 Calories; 20.8g Fat; 12g Carbs; 4.6g Protein; 4.6g Sugars

Ingredients

3 avocados, pitted, peeled and mashed
1 tablespoon vanilla extract
1 cup xylitol
1/8 teaspoon xanthan gum
1 teaspoon lemon juice
1 cup buttermilk
1 cup full-fat milk

Directions

- Mix all ingredients in your blender or a food processor until creamy, smooth and uniform. Let cool completely.

Storing

Spoon your pudding into six airtight containers; keep in your refrigerator for 5 to 6 days.
To freeze, spoon the pudding into plastic cups and insert wooden pop sticks into the center of each cup, if desired. Freeze up to 1 month. Defrost in the refrigerator. Enjoy!

175. Chocolate and Coconut Truffles

Ready in about 15 minutes + chilling time
Servings 16

When it comes to dessert tables, you cannot go wrong with truffles. These delectable balls look and taste wonderful!

Per serving: 90 Calories; 6.3g Fat; 4.9g Carbs; 3.7g Protein; 4g Sugars

Ingredients

1 ½ cups bittersweet chocolate, sugar-free, broken into chunks
4 tablespoons coconut, desiccated
1/2 stick butter
1 cup double cream
3 tablespoons xylitol
1/2 teaspoon pure almond extract
1 teaspoon vanilla paste
A pinch of salt
A pinch of freshly grated nutmeg
1 tablespoon cognac
1/4 cup unsweetened Dutch-processed cocoa powder

Directions

- Thoroughly combine the chocolate, coconut, butter, double cream, xylitol, almond extract, vanilla, salt, and grated nutmeg.
- Microwave for 1 minute on medium-high; let it cool slightly. Now, stir in cognac and vanilla.
- Place in your refrigerator for 2 hours. Shape the mixture into balls; roll each ball in cocoa powder.

Storing

Place chocolate truffles in airtight containers or Ziploc bags; keep in your refrigerator for 3 weeks to 1 month.
To freeze, arrange your truffles on a baking tray in a single layer; freeze for about 2 hours. Transfer the frozen truffles to an airtight container. Freeze for up to a month. Bon appétit!

176. Cheesy Coconut Cake

Ready in about 30 minutes
Servings 12

This cake mixes up fast and easy and bakes while you have dinner. It has a sophisticated flavor and lighter-than-air texture.

Per serving: 246 Calories; 22.2g Fat; 6.7g Carbs; 8.1g Protein; 1.9g Sugars

Ingredients

10 ounces almond meal
1 ounce coconut, shredded
1 teaspoon baking powder
1/8 teaspoon salt
4 eggs, lightly beaten
3 ounces stevia
1/2 stick butter
5 ounces coconut yogurt
5 ounces cream cheese

Directions

- Start by preheating your oven to 350 degrees F. Spritz 2 spring form pans with a nonstick cooking spray.
- In a mixing bowl, thoroughly combine the almond meal, coconut and baking powder. Stir in the salt, eggs and 2 ounces of stevia.
- Combine the 2 mixtures and stir until everything is well incorporated.
- Transfer the mixture into 2 spring form pans, introduce in the oven at 350 degrees F; bake for 20 to 25 minutes.
- Transfer to a wire rack to cool completely. In the meantime, mix the other ingredients, including the remaining 1 ounce of stevia.
- Place one cake layer on a plate; spread half of the cream cheese filling over it. Now, top with another cake layer; spread the rest of the cream cheese filling over the top.

Storing

Cover loosely with aluminum foil or plastic wrap and refrigerate for a week.
To freeze, place the cake on a baking pan and freeze for 2 hours. Now, wrap it in a foil and place in a freezer bag. It can be frozen for 2 to 3 months. Bon appétit!

177. Coconut Apple Cobbler

Ready in about 30 minutes
Servings 8

Warm apples topped with crispy topping makes a delicious fruit dessert! Kids of all ages will enjoy this cobbler.

Per serving: 152 Calories; 11.8g Fat; 10.7g Carbs; 2.5g Protein; 7.4g Sugars

Ingredients

2 ½ cups apples, cored and sliced
1/2 tablespoon fresh lemon juice
1/3 teaspoon xanthan gum
1 cup almond flour
1/4 cup coconut flour
3/4 cup xylitol
2 eggs, whisked
5 tablespoons coconut oil, melted

Directions

- Start by preheating your oven to 360 degrees F. Lightly grease a baking dish with a nonstick cooking spray.
- Arrange the apples on the bottom of the baking dish. Drizzle with lemon juice and xanthan gum.
- Then, in a mixing bowl, mix the flour with xylitol and eggs until the mixture resembles coarse meal. Spread this mixture over the apples.
- Drizzle coconut oil over topping. Bake for 25 minutes or until dough rises.

Storing

Place apple cobbler in four airtight containers; keep in your refrigerator for 4 to 5 days.
To freeze, place apple cobbler in four airtight containers or Ziploc bags; it can be frozen for 3 months. Defrost in your microwave for a few minutes. Bon appétit!

178. Cashew Butter Fat Bombs

Ready in about 40 minutes
Servings 12

These amazing balls will satisfy your nut craving! Many store-bought cashew butters contain an added sweetener so be careful or make your homemade one.

Per serving: 114 Calories; 10.6g Fat; 3.4g Carbs; 3.1g Protein; 0.3g Sugars

Ingredients

1/2 cup almonds
1/3 cup walnuts
1/2 cup cashew butter
1/2 stick butter
2 tablespoons cocoa powder, unsweetened
10 drops liquid stevia
1 teaspoon vanilla extract
1/4 cup unsweetened peanut flour

Directions

- Chop the almonds and walnuts in your food processor.
- Transfer to a mixing bowl; add the other ingredients.
- Scoop out tablespoons of batter onto a cookie sheet lined with a wax paper. Place in your freezer approximately 30 minutes to cool completely.

Storing

Place fat bombs in airtight containers or Ziploc bags; keep in your refrigerator for 10 days.
To freeze, arrange fat bombs on a baking tray in a single layer; freeze for about 2 hours. Transfer the frozen bombs to an airtight container. Freeze for up to 2 months. Bon appétit!

179. Chocolate Cake with Almond-Choc Ganache

Ready in about 50 minutes + chilling time
Servings 10

A decadent chocolate cake with nutty ganache, you'll want the moment to last forever.

Per serving: 313 Calories; 30.7g Fat; 7.5g Carbs; 7.3g Protein; 1g Sugars

Ingredients

1/2 cup water
3/4 cup granulated Swerve
14 ounces unsweetened chocolate chunks
2 sticks butter, cold
5 eggs
1/2 teaspoon pure almond extract
1/4 teaspoon ground nutmeg
1/4 teaspoon ground cardamom
A pinch of salt

For Almond-Choc Ganache:
3/4 cups double cream
9 ounces sugar-free dark chocolate, broken into chunks
1/4 cup smooth almond butter
A pinch of salt
1/2 teaspoon ginger powder
1/2 teaspoon cardamom powder

Directions

- Begin by preheating your oven to 360 degrees F. Line a baking pan with parchment paper.
- Now bring water to a rolling boil in a deep pan; add Swerve and cook until it is dissolved.
- Microwave the chocolate until melted. Add butter to the melted chocolate and beat with an electric mixer.
- Add the chocolate mixture to the hot water mixture. Now, add the eggs, one at a time, whipping continuously.
- Add almond extract, nutmeg, cardamom, and salt; stir well. Spoon the mixture into the prepared baking pan; wrap with foil.
- Lower the baking pan into a larger pan; add boiling water about 1 inch deep.
- Bake for 40 to 45 minutes. Allow it to cool completely before removing from the pan.
- Meanwhile, place double cream in a pan over a moderately high heat and bring to a boil. Pour hot cream over dark chocolate; whisk until chocolate is melted.
- Add the remaining ingredients for the ganache and whip until it is uniform and smooth. Finally, glaze a cooled cake.

Storing

Cover loosely with aluminum foil or plastic wrap and refrigerate for a week.
To freeze, place the cake on a baking pan and freeze for 2 hours; then, place in a heavy-duty freezer bag. It will maintain the best quality for about 4 to 6 months. Enjoy!

180. Quick Chocolate and Walnut Cookies

Ready in about 30 minutes
Servings 10

It's tea time! Whether you're on a keto diet or not, try these cookies with a cup of tea today!

Per serving: 157 Calories; 14.8g Fat; 3.5g Carbs; 4.5g Protein; 0.1g Sugars

Ingredients

1 stick butter
1/2 teaspoon pure almond extract
2 eggs
15 drops liquid stevia
1/8 teaspoon kosher salt
1 ¾ cups almond flour
1/2 teaspoon baking powder
1/4 teaspoon ground cinnamon
1/2 cup walnuts, chopped
1/3 cup sugar-free baker's chocolate, cut into chunks

Directions

- Heat the butter in a pan that is preheated over a moderate flame; stir and cook until it is browned.
- In a mixing bowl, beat the pure almond extract with the eggs, stevia, and salt.
- Add the melted butter, along with the other ingredients.
- Preheat your oven to 350 degrees F. Line a cookie sheet with a parchment paper. Spritz with a nonstick cooking spray.
- Bake for 25 minutes and transfer to a wire rack to cool completely.

Storing

Place your cookies in a tightly covered airtight container; keep in your refrigerator for 5 to 7 days.
To freeze, wrap cookies tightly with foil or place in heavy-duty freezer bag. It will maintain the best quality for about 6 to 8 months. Enjoy!

181. Walnut and White Chocolate Fudge

Ready in about 15 minutes + chilling time
Servings 12

For this fudge, don't overheat the butter and walnut butter, they should have a semi soft consistency. If you are able to, use a homemade walnut butter.

Per serving: 202 Calories; 21.3g Fat; 2.3g Carbs; 2.4g Protein; 0.6g Sugars

Ingredients

3/4 cup butter, softened
1 ¼ cups walnut butter, sugar-free
3 ounces sugar-free white chocolate
1/3 cup coconut milk, unsweetened
2 tablespoons xylitol
1/8 teaspoon coarse sea salt
1/4 teaspoon grated nutmeg
1/4 teaspoon ground star anise
1/4 teaspoon lemon peel zest

Directions

- Microwave butter, walnut butter, and white chocolate until they are melted. Add the butter mixture to your food processor.
- Now, add the other ingredients and mix again until everything is well incorporated. Scrape the mixture into a parchment lined baking pan.

Storing

Cover chocolate fudge with foil or plastic wrap to prevent drying out. It will last for about 1 to 2 days at room temperature.
Cover with aluminum foil or plastic wrap and refrigerate for a week.
To freeze, wrap chocolate fudge tightly with foil or place in a heavy-duty freezer bag. Freeze for up to 4 to 6 months. Enjoy!

182. Chocolate Cream Cheese Muffins

Ready in about 25 minutes
Servings 12

If you have just found out that you can make great keto muffins at home, you probably feel great! These muffins are so easy to make in your own kitchen and they follow keto principles.

Per serving: 134 Calories; 12.5g Fat; 3.3g Carbs; 4.6g Protein; 0.7g Sugars

Ingredients

7 tablespoons butter, melted
5 eggs
2 ounces cocoa powder
1 teaspoon pure vanilla extract
1 teaspoon maple flavor
1/3 teaspoon baking powder
6 ounces Neufchatel cheese, at room temperature
1/4 cup xylitol

Directions

- Beat all ingredients with an electric mixer.
- Place a paper baking cup in each of 12 muffin cups. Fill each cup 2/3 full.
- Bake at 360 degrees F about 23 minutes. Allow your muffins to cool completely.

Storing

Place the muffins in airtight containers and refrigerate for a week.
To freeze, place the muffins on a baking tray and freeze for 2 hours. Now, place them in airtight containers. They can be frozen for 2 to 3 months. Bon appétit!

183. The Best Walnut Truffles Ever

Ready in about 1 hour
Servings 10

Once shaped, these truffles can be rolled in unsweetened cocoa powder, coconut, matcha powder, and so forth. This is a great idea for the next party, just be sure to make a double batch!

Per serving: 162 Calories; 14.6g Fat; 5.9g Carbs; 2.3g Protein; 4.4g Sugars

Ingredients

1/2 stick butter
4 ounces heavy cream
1/4 cup Sukrin Icing
1 tablespoon brandy
1/2 teaspoon pure almond extract
1/2 cup chopped toasted walnuts
1/2 cup chocolate chips, sugar-free
4 tablespoons walnuts, coarsely chopped

Directions

- Melt the butter in a double boiler, stirring constantly.
- Then, stir in the cream and Sukrin icing; stir to combine well. Remove from heat and add brandy, almond extract and chopped walnuts.
- Now, allow it to cool at room temperature. Shape into 20 balls and chill for 40 to 50 minutes.
- In a double boiler, melt chocolate chips over medium-low heat. Dip each ball into the chocolate coating.
- Afterwards, roll your truffles in chopped walnuts.

Storing

Place your truffles in airtight containers or Ziploc bags; keep in your refrigerator for 3 weeks to 1 month. To freeze, arrange your truffles on a baking tray in a single layer; freeze for about 2 hours. Transfer the frozen truffles to an airtight container. Freeze for up to a month. Bon appétit!

184. Almond Dessert Bars

Ready in about 30 minutes
Servings 8

Almond lovers will love these fantastic low-carb dessert bars. This recipe is pretty adaptable. You can add walnuts and hazelnuts instead of almonds. You can add chunks of sugar-free chocolate too.

Per serving: 241 Calories; 23.6g Fat; 3.7g Carbs; 5.2g Protein; 0.4g Sugars

Ingredients

2 cups almond flour
3/4 teaspoon baking powder
1/2 cup Swerve
1/2 teaspoon ground cinnamon
A pinch of sea salt
A pinch of grated nutmeg
1 stick butter, melted
3 eggs
1/2 cup Swerve
1 teaspoon vanilla paste
3/4 cup heavy whipping cream
1/2 cup almonds, chopped

Directions

- Preheat your oven to 360 degrees F. Then, line a baking pan with parchment paper.
- In a mixing bowl, thoroughly combine almond flour, baking powder, Swerve, cinnamon, salt, and nutmeg.
- Now, stir in the melted butter, eggs, Swerve, and vanilla paste. Next, stir in the heavy cream to create a soft texture.
- Fold in the chopped almonds and gently stir until everything is well incorporated. Spoon the batter into the baking pan.
- Bake approximately 27 minutes. Allow it to cool completely and cut into bars.

Storing

Cover almond bars with foil or plastic wrap to prevent drying out. It will last for about 1 day at room temperature.
Cover with aluminum foil or plastic wrap and refrigerate for two weeks.
To freeze, wrap them tightly with foil or place in a heavy-duty freezer bag. Freeze for up to 3 to 4 months. Enjoy!

185. Festive Cake with Cream Cheese Frosting

Ready in about 40 minutes + chilling time
Servings 10

Konjac root fiber, also known as Konjac glucomannan powder, is a water-soluble fiber, it is also a gluten-free and fat-free ingredient. Some good alternatives are psyllium husk, agar-agar, and xanthan gum.

Per serving: 241 Calories; 22.6g Fat; 4.2g Carbs; 6.6g Protein; 2.9g Sugars

Ingredients

2/3 cup coconut flour
1 ½ cups almond flour
1/2 teaspoon baking soda
1/2 teaspoon baking powder
A pinch of salt
A pinch of grated nutmeg
1/2 teaspoon Konjac root fiber
1 cup Swerve
1 teaspoon fresh ginger, grated
2 ½ tablespoons ghee
4 eggs
1 cup coconut milk, sugar-free
1 teaspoon rum extract
1 teaspoon vanilla extract

For the Cream Cheese Frosting:
10 ounces cream cheese, cold
1/3 cup powdered granular sweetener
3 ounces butter, at room temperature
1 teaspoon vanilla
A few drops chocolate flavor

Directions

- Start by preheating your oven to 360 degrees F. Line a baking pan with parchment paper.
- In a mixing bowl, combine coconut flour, almond flour, baking soda, baking powder, salt, nutmeg, Konjac root fiber, Swerve, and ginger.
- Microwave ghee until melted and add to the dry mixture in the mixing bowl. Fold in the eggs, one at a time, and stir until combined.
- Lastly, pour in coconut milk, rum extract, and vanilla extract until your batter is light and fluffy.
- Press the mixture into the prepared baking pan. Bake for 28 to 33 minutes or until a cake tester inserted in center comes out clean and dry.
- Let it cool to room temperature.
- Meanwhile, beat the cream cheese with an electric mixer until smooth. Stir in powdered granular sweetener and beat again. Beat in the vanilla until it is completely incorporated.
- Add the butter, vanilla, and chocolate flavor; whip until light, fluffy and uniform. Frost the cake.

Storing

Cover loosely with aluminum foil or plastic wrap and refrigerate for a week.
To freeze, place the cake in a heavy-duty freezer bag. It will maintain the best quality for about 4 to 6 months. Enjoy!

186. Brownie Pecan Cupcakes

Ready in about 25 minutes
Servings 12

Here's a perfect dessert for any potluck! If there is something better than brownie cake then it's a brownie cupcake.

Per serving: 251 Calories; 21.5g Fat; 8.6g Carbs; 6.4g Protein; 4.3g Sugars

Ingredients

3/4 cup butter, melted
5 eggs
4 ounces cocoa powder
1/2 cup pecans, ground
1 teaspoon vanilla paste
3/4 teaspoon baking powder
1/4 teaspoon ground cloves
3 ounces cream cheese
3 ounces sour cream
2 tablespoons stevia powder

Directions

- Preheat your oven to 360 degrees F. Place a baking cup in each of 12 regular-size muffin cups.
- Thoroughly combine all ingredients in your food processor. Spoon the batter into the muffin cups.
- Bake for 18 to 22 minutes. Transfer to a wire rack to cool completely.

Storing

Divide your cupcakes between four airtight containers; keep in the refrigerator for 3 to 4 days.
For freezing, divide your cupcakes among four Ziploc bags and freeze up to 4 to 5 months. Defrost in your microwave for a couple of minutes. Enjoy!

187. Nutty Mother's Day Cake

Ready in about 30 minutes + chilling time
Servings 10

Make your keto dessert a little more excessive by adding crunchy toasted nuts. This is one of those cakes that taste better the second day.

Per serving: 211 Calories; 19g Fat; 4.4g Carbs; 7g Protein; 4.4g Sugars

Ingredients

For the Crust:
4 tablespoons peanut butter, room temperature
1 cup almond meal
2 tablespoons almonds, toasted and chopped

For the Filling:
10 ounces cream cheese, room temperature
2 eggs
1/2 teaspoon Stevia
1/2 teaspoon vanilla essence
1/2 teaspoon sugar-free caramel flavored syrup
1 teaspoon fresh ginger, grated
A pinch of salt
A pinch of grated nutmeg

Directions

- Begin by preheating your oven to 360 degrees F. Line a baking pan with parchment paper.
- Thoroughly combine peanut butter with almond meal. Then, press the crust mixture into your baking pan and bake for 7 minutes.
- Then, make the filling, by mixing all the filling ingredients with an electric mixer.
- Spread the filling onto the prepared crusts; bake for a further 18 minutes.
- Transfer it to the refrigerator to chill. Garnish with chopped, toasted almonds.

Storing

Cover the cake with a foil or plastic wrap to prevent drying out; refrigerate for a week.
To freeze, place the cake in a heavy-duty freezer bag or wrap it tightly with aluminum foil. It will maintain the best quality for about 4 to 6 months. Enjoy!

188. Avocado and Peanut Butter Pudding

Ready in about 15 minutes
Servings 4

This nutritionally dense pudding is naturally sweetened with stevia and enriched with crunchy peanut butter. For this pudding, use ripe avocados that are soft but still firm.

Per serving: 288 Calories; 27.3g Fat; 8.9g Carbs; 6.2g Protein; 2.4g Sugars

Ingredients

1 ½ cups avocado, peeled, pitted, and diced
1/2 cup crunchy peanut butter
50 drops liquid stevia
1/2 cup canned coconut milk
1 teaspoon pure vanilla extract
1/4 teaspoon ground cloves
1 tablespoon lime juice
1/2 cup coconut whipped cream

Directions

- Process avocados, peanut butter, stevia and coconut milk in a blender.
- Now, add vanilla extract, cloves, and lime juice. Garnish with coconut whipped cream.

Storing

Spoon your pudding into four airtight containers; keep in your refrigerator for 5 to 6 days.
To freeze, place your pudding in four airtight containers. You can also spoon the pudding into plastic cups and insert wooden pop sticks into the center of each cup. Freeze up to 1 month.
Defrost in the refrigerator. Enjoy!

189. Caramel Macchiato Candies

Ready in about 10 minutes + chilling time
Servings 8

Once you taste how good these candies are, they will become a must make dessert! These candies are kid friendly and guilt-free.

Per serving: 145 Calories; 12.8g Fat; 6.9g Carbs; 0.9g Protein; 6.1g Sugars

Ingredients

3 tablespoons cocoa butter
3 tablespoons butter
3 ounces dark chocolate, sugar-free
1 teaspoon cold brew coffee concentrate
1 teaspoon sugar-free caramel flavored syrup
6 drops liquid stevia

Directions

- Microwave cocoa butter, butter, and chocolate for 1 minute or so.
- Stir in the remaining ingredients. Pour into candy-safe molds.

Storing

Layer candies in an airtight container between sheets of waxed paper; refrigerate for 10 days.
For freezing, place them in sealed airtight containers. Freeze up to 6 to 9 months. Enjoy!

190. Cheesecake Cupcakes with Vanilla Frosting

Ready in about 30 minutes + chilling time
Servings 8

These silky-smooth cupcakes literally melt on your tongue. Kids will be thrilled!

Per serving: 165 Calories; 15.6g Fat; 8.4g Carbs; 5.2g Protein; 0.2g Sugars

Ingredients

For the Muffins:
3 tablespoons coconut oil
10 ounces Ricotta cheese, at room temperature
1 tablespoon rum
2 eggs
2 packets stevia
1/8 teaspoon ground cloves
1/4 teaspoon ground cinnamon
1/8 teaspoon nutmeg, preferably freshly grated

For the Frosting:
1/2 cup confectioners' Swerve
1/2 stick butter, softened
1 teaspoon vanilla
1 ½ tablespoons full-fat milk

Directions

- Preheat your oven to 360 degrees F; coat muffin cups with cupcake liners.
- Thoroughly combine coconut oil, Ricotta cheese, rum, eggs, stevia, cloves, cinnamon and nutmeg in your food processor.
- Scrape the batter into the muffin tin; bake for 13 to 16 minutes. Now, place in the freezer for 2 hours.
- In the meantime, combine confectioners' Swerve with butter and vanilla with an electric mixer.
- Slowly pour in milk in order to make a spreadable mixture. Frosts chilled cheesecake cupcakes.

Storing

Place the cupcakes in airtight containers and refrigerate for a week.
To freeze, place the cupcakes on a baking tray and freeze for 2 hours. Now, place them in airtight containers. They can be frozen for 2 to 3 months. Bon appétit!

191. Simple Strawberry Scones

Ready in about 25 minutes
Servings 10

Just like the name says, these scones are simple, fruity and chewy. Further, they have zero sugar, as well as less saturated fat and fewer carbs than classic ones. How could it be any better than this?

Per serving: 245 Calories; 21.6g Fat; 10.4g Carbs; 3.8g Protein; 0.8g Sugars

Ingredients

1 cup coconut flour
1 cup almond flour
1 teaspoon baking powder
A pinch of salt
1 cup strawberries
2 eggs
1 ½ sticks butter
1 cup heavy cream
10 tablespoons liquid stevia
1 teaspoon vanilla extract

Directions

- Start by preheating your oven to 350 degrees F.
- In a mixing bowl, thoroughly combine the flour with baking powder, salt and strawberries.
- In another mixing bowl, beat the eggs with butter and cream. Stir in liquid stevia and vanilla extract; stir to combine well.
- Combine the 2 mixtures and stir until you obtain a soft dough. Knead gently and avoid overworking your dough.
- Shape into 16 triangles and arrange on a lined baking sheet; bake for 18 minutes.

Storing

Place your scones in airtight containers and refrigerate for a week.
Freeze the scones on a baking tray until they are solid; place them in airtight containers and freeze for up to 3 months.

192. Coconut Creamsicle Chia Pudding

Ready in about 20 minutes
Servings 4

Sometimes the best dessert recipes are not difficult at all. You can fix up this pudding in advance because it can be stored in your refrigerator up to 3 days.

Per serving: 226 Calories; 17.9g Fat; 11g Carbs; 5.9g Protein; 5g Sugars

Ingredients

1 cup water
1 cup heavy cream
1 cup coconut milk, unsweetened
1 teaspoon vanilla extract
1 cup chia seeds
1/4 cup coconut shreds, unsweetened
2 tablespoons erythritol
1/4 teaspoon ground cloves
1/2 teaspoon ground anise star

Directions

- Thoroughly combine all of the above ingredients in a mixing dish.
- Allow it to stand at least 20 minutes, stirring periodically. Let cool completely.

Storing

Divide the pudding among four airtight containers; refrigerate for 3 days.
To freeze, pour the mixture into ice-pop molds. Cover and insert sticks. Freeze until firm, at least 4 hours. Dip molds briefly in hot water to release pops. Freeze up to 1 month. Enjoy!

193. Berry and Coconut Cup Smoothie

Ready in about 10 minutes
Servings 4

There's no such thing as a bowl of a thick and rich berry smoothie. We added an almond butter to achieve a better, silky texture but you can use peanut or walnut butter as well.

Per serving: 274 Calories; 26.8g Fat; 7.5g Carbs; 3.9g Protein; 3.2g Sugars

Ingredients

1/2 cup raspberries, frozen
1 cup coconut milk
2 tablespoons almond butter
1/4 cup coconut shreds
1 teaspoon vanilla paste
4 drops liquid stevia
2 tablespoons hemp seeds

Directions

- Pulse frozen berries in your food processor to desired consistency.
- Add coconut milk, almond butter, coconut, vanilla and stevia. Blend until everything is well incorporated; top with hemp seeds

Storing

Pour the mixture into four glass containers with airtight lids; make sure to fill the containers to the very top. Seal your containers tightly and store in the refrigerator for up to 24 hours.
To freeze, pour the mixture into freezer-safe jars. They will maintain the best quality for 3 months. Defrost in your refrigerator.

194. Coconut and Peanut Butter Flan

Ready in about 40 minutes + chilling time
Servings 4

Flan is a light an elegant dessert for a weeknight treat or to serve as a midnight snack. For the best ketogenic experience, make sure to use a homemade peanut butter.

Per serving: 304 Calories; 27.7g Fat; 6.6g Carbs; 11.6g Protein; 3.1g Sugars

Ingredients

1 cup coconut cream, unsweetened
4 eggs
1/2 cup peanut butter
1/2 cup granulated Swerve
1/4 teaspoon ground mace
1/2 teaspoon pure vanilla extract
1/2 teaspoon pure almond extract

Directions

- Begin by preheating your oven to 340 degrees F. Place 4 ramekins in a deep baking pan. Pour boiling water to a depth of about 1 inch.
- In a saucepan, bring coconut cream to a simmer. In a mixing dish, whisk the remaining ingredients until eggs are foamy.
- Slowly and gradually pour egg mixture into warm coconut cream, whisking constantly.
- Spoon the mixture into prepared ramekins and bake for 35 minutes, or until a tester comes out dry. Allow it to cool about 4 hours.

Storing

Divide the mixture among four airtight containers; it can be stored in the refrigerator up to 3 days.
Slide the flan into pieces; transfer them to a heavy-duty freezer bag. Store in your freezer up to 1 month. Defrost in the refrigerator. Bon appétit!

195. Christmas Walnut Penuche

Ready in about 2 hours
Servings 8

Make this crunchy, buttery penuche in your own kitchen! You can use these wonderfully inspirational sweets to create DIY presents for Christmas.

Per serving: 167 Calories; 17.1g Fat; 8.8g Carbs; 2.4g Protein; 7g Sugars

Ingredients

1 cup xylitol
1 cup condensed milk, unsweetened
1 stick butter
1/2 teaspoon vanilla paste
2 ounces toasted walnuts, chopped
1/4 teaspoon orange rind, grated
A pinch of salt

Directions

- Combine xylitol and milk in a pan that is preheated over a moderate heat. Simmer, stirring often, for 5 to 6 minutes.
- Stir in butter and vanilla. Cream with an electric mixer at low speed; beat until very creamy.
- Fold in chopped walnuts, orange rind, and salt; stir again. Afterwards, spoon into a baking dish and freeze until firm, about 2 hours.

Storing

Place dessert in airtight containers. Keep in your refrigerator for up to two weeks.
To freeze, wrap and package the pieces; place in the airtight container. Freeze up to 3 to 4 months. Bon appétit!

196. Cappuccino Ice Candy

Ready in about 10 minutes + chilling time
Servings 8

Have you ever wondered how delicious avocado, espresso, and heavy cream can be together? Try this recipe and you will be delighted!

Per serving: 117 Calories; 11.2g Fat; 5g Carbs; 1.3g Protein; 1.4g Sugars

Ingredients

1 ½ cups avocado, pitted, peeled and mashed
1 cup brewed espresso
2 tablespoons cocoa powder
1 cup heavy whipping cream
3 tablespoons erythritol
1/2 teaspoon cappuccino flavor extract
A pinch of salt
A pinch of grated nutmeg

Directions

- Throw all of the above ingredients into your food processor; mix until everything is well combined.
- Pour the mixture into an ice cube tray. Freeze overnight, at least 6 hours.

Storing

Place dessert in airtight containers. Keep in your refrigerator for up to 8 days.
Place in a heavy-duty freezer bag. Freeze up to 3 to 4 months. Bon appétit!

197. Decadent Pistachio Truffles

Ready in about 25 minutes + chilling time
Servings 6

Indulge in these melt-in-your-mouth truffles bursting with toasted pistachios. It is wonderful for potlucks, family gatherings and holidays!

Per serving: 113 Calories; 8.5g Fat; 8.9g Carbs; 1.7g Protein; 0.4g Sugars

Ingredients

3 bars sugar-free chocolate spread
1/2 cup heavy cream
1 teaspoon vanilla essence
1/4 teaspoon ground cinnamon
1/2 cup toasted pistachios, finely chopped

Directions

- Melt chocolate spread with heavy cream in your microwave for 1 minute or so.
- Add the vanilla and ground cinnamon; transfer to your refrigerator for 8 hours or until firm enough to shape.
- Shape the chocolate mixture into balls. Freeze for 20 minutes. Afterwards, roll the balls into the chopped pistachios.

Storing

Place your truffles in airtight containers or Ziploc bags; keep in your refrigerator for 3 weeks to 1 month. To freeze, arrange your truffles on a baking tray in a single layer; freeze for about 2 hours. Transfer the frozen truffles to an airtight container. Freeze for up to a month. Bon appétit!

198. Butterscotch Ice Cream

Ready in about 15 minutes + chilling time
Servings 8

Creamy and flavorsome, this is the perfect dessert for a hot summer day. It scoops well after freezing too.

Per serving: 89 Calories; 9.3g Fat; 1.5g Carbs; 0.8g Protein; 0.5g Sugars

Ingredients

3/4 cup heavy cream
1/2 cup coconut milk
1 tablespoon butterscotch flavoring
25 drops liquid stevia
1/3 teaspoon pure vanilla extract
A pinch of salt
1/4 cup sour cream

Directions

- Cook the heavy cream and coconut milk in a pan that is preheated over a medium-low flame. Let it simmer, stirring constantly, until there are no lumps.
- Allow it to cool at room temperature; mix in the remaining ingredients.
- Blend with an electric mixer until your desired consistency is reached.

Storing

Spoon your ice cream in an airtight container. Store your ice cream in the very back of the freezer. Freeze up to 2 to 4 months. Bon appétit!

199. Chocolate Lover's Dream Fudge

Ready in about 15 minutes + chilling time
Servings 8

This dessert is chock-full of rich low-carb chocolate, thick cream, and condensed milk. Did you know that National Fudge Day is June 16?

Per serving: 220 Calories; 20g Fat; 7g Carbs; 1.7g Protein; 1.4g Sugars

Ingredients

1 cup condensed milk, sugar-free
3/4 Sukrin chocolate, broken into pieces
1 stick butter
2 tablespoons coconut oil
4-5 drops Stevia
1/2 cup heavy cream

Directions

- Microwave condensed milk and Sukrin chocolate for 70 seconds; spoon into a baking dish and freeze until firm.
- Melt butter in a small-sized pan; stir in melted coconut oil, Stevia, and heavy cream; whisk to combine well or beat with a hand mixer.
- Spread the cream mixture over the fudge layer in the baking dish. Then, freezer until solid.

Storing

Cover your fudge with foil or plastic wrap to prevent drying out. It will last for about 1 to 2 days at room temperature.
Place in airtight containers and refrigerate for a week.
To freeze, wrap your fudge tightly with foil or place in heavy-duty freezer bags. Freeze for up to 4 to 6 months. Bon appétit!

200. Peanut Butter Cup Cookies

Ready in about 40 minutes
Servings 10

Get all of the rich flavors of peanut butter cake in these bite-sized pecan pie cookies. If you prefer an extra-silky texture, use a smooth peanut butter instead.

Per serving: 266 Calories; 28.1g Fat; 2.6g Carbs; 3.3g Protein; 1.2g Sugars

Ingredients

1/2 cup coconut oil
1/2 cup butter
1/2 cup crunchy peanut butter
3 tablespoons heavy cream
1 tablespoon granular Swerve

Directions

- Simmer all of the above ingredients in a pan over medium-low heat; stir continuously until everything is well incorporated.
- Divide the batter among muffin cups lined with cupcake wrappers. Allow them to harden at least 30 minutes in your freezer.

Storing

Divide cup cookies between four airtight containers; keep in the refrigerator for 3 to 4 days.
For freezing, divide your cup cookies between four Ziploc bags and freeze up to 4 to 5 months. Defrost in the refrigerator. Enjoy!

Made in the USA
Middletown, DE
05 August 2018